Hearts and Minds

foreword by
CHARLES COLSON

hearts and minds

*Raising your child
with a Christian view
of the world*

Kenneth Boa
John Alan Turner

 Tyndale House Publishers, Inc. Carol Stream, Illinois

Visit Tyndale's exciting Web site at www.tyndale.com

TYNDALE and Tyndale's quill logo are registered trademarks of Tyndale House Publishers, Inc.

Hearts and Minds: Raising Your Child with a Christian View of the World

Copyright © 2006 by Kenneth Boa and John Alan Turner. All rights reserved.

Cover photo copyright © by Dag Sundberg/Getty Images. All rights reserved.

Designed by Luke Daab

Edited by Linda Schlafer

Library of Congress Cataloging-in-Publication Data

Boa, Kenneth.
    Hearts and minds : raising your child with a Christian view of the world / Kenneth Boa and John Alan Turner.
       p. cm.
    Includes bibliographical references.
    ISBN-13: 978-1-4143-0164-8 (sc : alk. paper)
    ISBN-10: 1-4143-0164-2 (sc : alk. paper)
    1. Parents—Religious life. 2. Christianity—Philosophy. 3. Parenting—Religious aspects—Christianity. 4. Child rearing—Religious aspects—Christianity. I. Turner, John Alan. II. Title.
    BV4529.B62 2006
    248.8′45—dc22   2006014554

Printed in the United States of America

12 11 10 09 08 07 06
 7 6 5 4 3 2 1

*Finding a good wife is a blessing.
Finding a good wife who is also a good
mother is an even greater blessing.
Finding a good wife who is also a good
mother and a lover of God is the greatest
blessing of all. So, it is with love and
gratitude that we dedicate this book
to our wives, Karen and Jill.*

Contents

Foreword

A recent network television special on American evangelicals included some remarkably sympathetic interviews. One woman, however, jarred me with comments that probably are shared by millions of Christian parents. She said she was so busy running the kids to soccer matches, helping them with their homework, cooking meals, driving to her part-time job, and looking after her husband that, by day's end, she couldn't even care "what's going on in the world."

With my own children raising teenagers, I could understand. But I couldn't help wondering what this mother will be able to say when her son comes home from high school biology class to tell her that we evolved from the primordial soup—that through billions of years of natural selection we've arrived at our present state. And how will she respond when her daughter comes home from her college philosophy class bewildered because her professor announced there is no such thing as truth. And if her children are asked to participate in their school's Day of Silence in support of the homosexual agenda, will she know how to explain why this agenda is both deceitful and destructive?

If this mother thought about it for a minute, she'd realize that she cannot afford *not* to take time to learn what the world is teaching her kids, and then learn how to counteract it with bracing doses of Christian worldview instruction. Otherwise, her children may eventually lose their faith as they encounter competing worldviews in college or at work.

That's why I am so delighted that my longtime friend and associate Kenneth Boa and my new friend John Alan Turner have written a book that challenges parents to go beyond behavior modification in their children, to stop settling for the false positives of sleeping through the night or sitting still at the dinner table, and raise the bar of parenting to God's standard. They believe—and rightfully so—that God's agenda for children is that they grow up to become like Jesus, not just in Christlike conduct, but in Christlike thoughts, values, and attitudes.

Ken and John have presented an aggressive agenda in this book. They are convinced, as I am, that the church's most urgent priority today is equipping this generation to defend their faith in the marketplace of ideas, and to make a winsome defense of moral truth.

So in this book, Ken and John give parents the basic tools they need to shape the way a child sees God, the world, and their place in the world, so those children can help advance the borders of God's kingdom here on earth. With a steady stream of logic, real-life stories, and common sense, they equip parents with the nuts and bolts of a Christian worldview in terms that parents can understand, so they can transfer that framework to their children before launching them out into the world to change it for God's sake.

Perhaps what is most exciting about this book is how Ken and John take weighty concepts and distill them into clear and precise terms. This is not a book for the academic elite (though there is much to be gained here). Rather, this is a book for regular, everyday parents, the busy and overworked dad, and that poor, harried soccer mom I mentioned earlier.

And what a difference we can make if we give our children the tools they need to defend their faith. I am reminded of the story about a young college student who was coached by a graduate of Prison Fellowship's Centurions Program, a woman named Nancy Fitzgerald. For years, Nancy has taught a Christian worldview course, which she now calls Anchors Away, in her Indianapolis home. Her basement is packed every Sunday night with high school seniors. Nancy told me about an encounter that one of her Anchors Away graduates had with a college ethics professor who challenged his students with the classic Heinz Dilemma: that is, how do you choose one person to eliminate from a crowded lifeboat, thereby saving the others?

Nancy's student refused to participate in classroom discussions, claiming that choosing one person to die is immoral and offended her Christian conscience. Furious, her professor threatened to flunk her if she didn't participate. But she held her ground.

Something about this girl's moral stance intrigued the professor in spite of himself. He ultimately gave her an A and asked her to explain her beliefs to the whole class. And, if you can imagine it, the professor eventually became a Christian.

Most Christian kids, without worldview training, will not be able to handle themselves this well at college. As part of my own teaching program, I speak to several youth groups a year. I always start by asking if there's such a thing as absolute truth. Hardly a hand goes up. After I've given several obvious illustrations (for example, if a little old lady asks for help crossing the street, it would be—always and everywhere—immoral to push her in front of a bus), their eyes pop open as they realize that the moral truth is written on their hearts (Romans 2). It's an "Aha!" moment.

The call to equip ourselves, and our children, with moral truth is a biblical mandate. It's what Peter meant when he said we must be prepared to give a reason for the hope that is in us (1 Peter 3:15). We mustn't fail in this endeavor. That harried young mother in the NBC special, too busy to teach her kids where secular worldviews are wrong—that's just what the enemies of Christianity want to hear. And it's why you and I must get serious about learning and teaching worldview. If we do, I'm convinced we can save our children—literally.

And then our kids will learn, as Francis Schaeffer used to say, how to become worldview missionaries to their own culture, fulfilling the Great Commission and the cultural commission in their own generation.

Chuck Colson

Acknowledgments

From Ken Boa:

Through the grace of God, I have been blessed all my life with a rich tapestry of treasured relationships. These people, too numerous to name, have shaped, encouraged, guided, and taught me throughout the course of my journey. Because of the nature of this book, I want to give particular thanks not only for my parents, Kenneth and Ruthelaine, who are now with the Lord, but also to others who participated in the process of parenting me. My extraordinary grandmother, Lottie Mae Bacle Kelley, shaped my spiritual journey more than any other person, and our reunion will be a joy. I also think of my uncle and aunt, Roland and Ann Kelley, with profound gratitude for their abiding impact on my life, and of David and Roxie Haines for their palpable model of what it means to walk with Christ.

"Remember those who led you, who spoke the word of God to you; and considering the result of their conduct, imitate their faith." (Hebrews 13:7, NASB)

From John Alan Turner:

This book has been part of my life for nearly two-and-a-half years, from initial outline to final, last-minute corrections. Many people helped at points along the way—and their help was immeasurable.

First of all, my thanks to the people at the reThink Group. You gave me the time and space I needed to complete my work on this manuscript. Thanks especially to Jeff Sandstrom, Leigha Montgomery, Sue Miller, and Kristi Lemoine. Thanks to Melanie Williams, Jennifer Rebecca Van Ypren "Flexible" Tamborello, and Greg Payne for not getting angry when I missed other deadlines to make this one. Special thanks also to Reggie Joiner. I've learned so much from you about communication, strategy, and how to talk to parents in ways they can understand.

Anne-Geri Fann, nobody knows how to land a chapter like you. Without your help, this book would never have ended.

Tony Myles, you're a quick learner, a creative thinker, and a fine writer. Your insights brought clarity to several chapters.

Jeff Scott (the preacher not the singer), you helped me work through several chapters when I was stuck in the doldrums. Because of you, I was able to quote The Beatles, Tina Turner, and William Law in the same chapter—one of my proudest achievements.

Phil Pierce, you are one of the funniest men I've ever known. Your friendship is a joy to me.

Rick Hazelip, you are one of the godliest men I've ever known. Your partnership has already made Faith 2.0 successful.

Sandra Morales, you never fail to remind me that I'm not that smart, and that you knew me when I parted my hair in the middle and blew it dry. For that, I'll be eternally grateful.

Many friends had to sit and listen to me talk about the writing of this book. You were all unusually gracious and patient. To name only two is to overlook the majority, but Dane Booth and David Blackwell deserve special mention. Because of you, I have a clearer conscience and a license to say things I would never have said otherwise.

My heartfelt gratitude goes to all the people who gave me personal stories to include in this book: Bob Russell, Lanny Donoho, Stuart Hall, Brian McLaren, Bob and Jennifer Nahrstadt. Your stories will make this book real for many parents.

The Wednesday Night Bible Study I teach at the North Atlanta Church of Christ is the highlight of my week. You have learned the good, the bad, and the ugly about me and my family, and you love us anyway. Thanks for your prayers on this journey.

Thanks to all the readers of my blog who contributed comments on the subject of parenting—from the sublime to the ridiculous. We all remain "in his big grip."

Thanks also to a quartet of guys who read many of the chapters and made very helpful suggestions: Nino Elliott, Don McLaughlin, David Hutchens, and Steven Allen. You're all busy, but you made time for this project. Thanks for your help.

Jon Farrar, Linda Schlafer, and Dave Lindstedt, you made

completion of the book so much easier. You always responded quickly, and never got angry when I did not. Thanks for your flexibility and generosity.

Four more people, and we're done.

There is a lady in her eighties named Dona Cornutt, who lives in Pampa, Texas. If it weren't for her, I might not have given much thought to becoming a writer. Thank you, Dona. I made it!

Hal Runkel, you put me on the path to being a better parent and being a better writer about parenting. Your work inspires me to be the best I can be and spread the message of ScreamFree living to others.

Dr. B., thank you for offering me the chance to write this book with you. I often tell people that being friends with you is like being friends with C. S. Lewis. That's not true. Being friends with you is like being friends with Jesus.

And then there's my wife, Jill. You learned most of this stuff right along with me. You certainly wrote most of this stuff right along with me. You're not only my editor, you're my best friend and my partner in all things. You're the only person I want to partner with in parenting the three beautiful girls God has given us.

Introduction

Jeff Sandstrom, a Dove Award–winning music producer, grew up going to camp every summer. A Christian organization near his home in up-state New York hosted a summer camp for boys, designed to train them to be Christian leaders. In that time and place, being a Christian leader meant knowing how to lead congregational singing, stand in front of an audience, and preach.

One of the main events each summer was for these young boys to memorize prewritten, three-minute sermonettes and recite them for the rest of the camp on parent-visitation day. There were hundreds of these mini-homilies—with titles such as "Why Ivory Soap Floats" and "What Christ Did for Sinful Men"—and whoever could recite the most sermonettes verbatim, would gain admittance to the Hall of Fame.

Jeff Sandstrom desperately wanted his name in the Hall of Fame. His father was an associate pastor at their church. He led worship and the youth group, and the Sandstrom family was a pillar of the congrega-tion. As a pastor's son, there was some pressure on Jeff to act in certain ways and to know certain things. Everyone just knew that Jeff would leave camp that summer as the newest member of the Hall of Fame.

They did not expect Timmy Tollison to be as good as he proved to be.*

Timmy was a memorizing machine. It quickly became clear to everyone at camp that he was better than Jeff at reciting the sermonettes. He was likely going to be admitted into the Hall of Fame first and steal all of Jeff's thunder.

This is how it came about that on a muggy summer morning in the early 1980s, Jeff Sandstrom prayed, "Dear Jesus, please do not let Timmy Tollison remember 'What Christ Did for Sinful Men.'"

It's a good thing we grow out of that kind of childish behavior, isn't it?

*Timmy Tollison is not the boy's real name. We have changed the name to protect the innocent. Jeff Sandstrom's name has not been changed, because he told us we could use his story, and he was not innocent.

The July 19, 1996, issue of *USA Today* carried a story from Dadeville, Alabama, about a Bible-quoting contest gone wrong. Gabel Taylor and another man began an informal match to see who could quote the most Bible verses. Eventually, as in all such contests, one man bested the other. Thirty-eight-year-old Gabel Taylor was the victor. The other man, whose name was not revealed in the news article, got a gun and shot and killed Gabel Taylor.

Beyond making us laugh or wince, these two stories illustrate how important it is to define success properly for our children.

In this book, we're going to talk about how we as parents should live. We're not going to talk very much about how children ought to behave, although there will be some of that. Instead, we're going to cut straight to the heart of the matter and help you understand why it's more important to focus on what's happening inside your child than on what your child is doing.

Our goal is to help you train your children to think about and see the world in a certain way, and we firmly believe that their behavior will adjust itself accordingly. We are convinced that people usually act as they do because of what they believe. We're also convinced that parents who are overly concerned with external results (i.e., behavior) can turn out a lot of false positives—children who look great on the outside but whose insides are corrupt; children who do the right thing only until no one is looking. We may think that our children are on the right track because they attend church and know their memory verses, but the truth about a person's character eventually reveals itself, often with devastating results. Ask Gabel Taylor's family.

We've intentionally avoided techniques or gimmicks for making your children behave better. We have tried not to get bogged down in external measures that can produce a false sense of success for parents. This is not a book about how our children ought to behave, but about how we ought to live as their parents.

We built this book on a foundation laid by researchers and theologians, experts in the fields of psychology and education, such as Hal Runkel, Kevin Leman, Alfie Kohn, Ray Guarendi, Tim Kimmel, Edward Hallowell, and many others. We read a lot of books during the process of writing this one to be sure that our opinions were sound.

One of the biggest flaws we've found in many parenting books (especially Christian parenting books) is the myth of technique. Often the impression is given that we can control our children with the proper technique. This usually comes from misreading Proverbs 22:6: "Train a child in the way he should go, and when he is old he will not turn from it." The truth is that you cannot really control your children.

If your goal is to make your children behave in a certain way or to force them to be a certain kind of person, you may or may not achieve that goal. Kids grow up to be adults with minds of their own. You may do everything right and still see your kids walk away from their faith when they get older. Despite what you may have been led to believe, they may not come back. If your definition of successful parenting is having faithful children who make you proud and turn your friends green with envy, you may be setting yourself up for a rude awakening.

The truth is that you can't control your kids or their choices. The only person you can really control is yourself, and most of us struggle with that. What if we took Gary Thomas's advice? He says, "The ultimate issue is no longer how proud my children make me, but how faithful I've been to discharge the duties God has given me."[1] Focusing on our God-given responsibilities as parents changes our definition of success.

Parenting our kids requires gifts and skills that we don't have. Only God has what it takes to raise children properly, and he calls us to parent in partnership with him because he knows that it will make us rely more on him. As we are invited to draw closer to him each step of the way, parenting becomes a spiritually formative activity. We need to raise children as much as they need us to raise them.

We don't know many parents who feel completely competent in their role. When you find out that you're expecting a child, it changes who you are and how you live. How you live out the principles of a biblical worldview in the presence of your children will either help them or hinder them in their quest to connect with God.

The stakes are high because how parents live today will shape the world for the next generation. Our children will inherit the world that we bequeath to them. But don't let that discourage you. God is prepared to equip you for the task at hand.

Better Parenting or Better Parents?
How would you answer if you were asked, "Are you better at being a Christian or at being a parent?" Most of us would say that being a good Christian is a snap compared to being a good parent. Most of

us think of ourselves as decent Christians. The basics of Christianity are relatively easy to get a grip on, and they have remained constant for centuries. We have plenty of areas that we're working on, but God has helped us and brought us to where we are spiritually, so we feel relatively certain that he will continue to work in us.

But being a good parent? With all the talk shows and seminars out there, some of us feel that we must rely on the insight and education of professionally licensed and board-certified experts because they know more about our children than we do. It's difficult to master even the basics of parenting because there seem to be more basics now than there used to be.

Here's a secret that you may not have heard: Personhood sets the tone for parenthood.[2] In other words, *the kind of person you are will have a longer-lasting effect on your children than your parenting techniques.* Whether or not you were able to insightfully discern the inner monologue of your preteen daughter will not matter as much as whether or not you were an example of Christlikeness to her. If you want to be a better parent, the place to begin is with your own relationship with God. The closer you draw to him, the more transformed you will be by the power of the Holy Spirit; the more you take on God's perspective, the better you will be at parenting.

The proliferation of parenting books at the local bookstore can be overwhelming, and parents can begin to feel doubtful, anxious, and guilty. The last thing we want to do is to make parents feel more intimidated. God has called you to do something remarkable—to live in such a way that your child will see God and his purpose for each of us. That purpose is to bring glory to God by living with integrity, enjoying the gifts he gives us, and being good stewards of those gifts.

Chief among those gifts are our children. Part of living a God-honoring life is remembering that children are a blessing from God—however much they may sometimes feel like part of the Curse! One of the best things you can do for your child is to become the kind of person who feels good when you're told, "She's just like you." Instead of telling your son, "I can't wait until you have one just like you," what would it be like to say, "I hope you have a son who is as much of a blessing to you as you have been to me"?

It might also be helpful for you to know that the basics you need to be a good Christian are the same basics you need to be a good parent.

To be a good Christian you need to have the right beliefs, the right values, and the right practices. In other words, you must love God with your head, your heart, and your hands. As you do that, God's Spirit will transform you into a godly person, and your parenting will change as well.

There are other good books that deal with how to get your child to sleep through the night or sit still at the dinner table. We're more concerned with how you can help your children to see the world as it really is, to understand the world and their place in it, and to give them a filter through which they can interpret life as it is happening.

Your worldview shows up in why you vote, what you watch, where you shop, and how you drive. Your worldview determines how you talk to yourself and others, how you treat your neighbors, and whether or not you can forgive your enemies. Your worldview is demonstrated by your thoughts, feelings, words, and actions.

Here's the scary part: If you say you believe one thing but your behavior reveals something completely opposite, guess what your kids will remember.

That's why we're going to focus less on children and more on parents; less on child rearing and more on how parents can live in a way that demonstrates a life of faith to their children.

An Overview of the Book
In part 1, we will talk about families as the basic building blocks of society. As families go, so goes society—not the other way around. Therefore, if something has gone wrong with society, it is precisely because something has gone terribly wrong in our families. If we are ever going to stem the tide of moral decay in our world, we must begin at the family level.

Several factors make this difficult to do. In chapter 1, we'll consider the challenge of parenting in an age of specialization, and we'll make the case that parents must stop outsourcing their children's faith development. During the past couple of generations, the faith development of children has become church-based and home-supported. According to the biblical paradigm, however, it's supposed to be home-based and church-supported.

Parents are often afraid to take ownership of the faith-development process. It can be a daunting task; but with a simple understanding of the typical stages of faith development, parents can devise age-appropriate strategies. In chapter 2, we'll walk through four basic stages of faith development and give some practical examples of the things you can do at each stage to smooth the transitions your child will naturally go through.

One idea in this first section that isn't usually part of parenting discussions—even of biblical parenting—is using Jesus as our example. We tend to think that because Jesus did not have children, he doesn't have much to say about how we parent. In chapter 3, we'll look at Jesus' relationship with his disciples to glean some tips for teaching and training our children.

In part 2, we'll begin the heavy lifting. We'll unpack the basics of a Christian worldview in a way that busy dads and even-busier moms can understand. We hope it will help that we are both busy dads ourselves.

In chapter 4, we address the basic questions that a worldview seeks to answer, such as, Who am I? Where am I? How did I get here? Why am I here? What's wrong with me and my world? and, Is there a solution to the problems of this life? We can tell our children what we believe, but the way we live reveals more about our faith than our words ever will. If our lives were congruent with what we say we believe, the whole world would change.

Everything begins and ends with our concept of God. Either he exists or he does not. If he is who he says he is, then he defines reality. If our children are convinced that God exists and that he is not silent, more than half the battle is over. Chapter 5 deals with the importance of giving our children an accurate picture of God.

Once we grasp the fact that God exists and has revealed himself and his will to us, we can begin to piece together some answers to questions about meaning, purpose, and destiny. Chapter 6 presses the premise of God's character to its logical conclusions and shows how God's existence and his revealed will affect the other fundamental life questions.

Part 3 examines what we value as Christians. There is a wrong-headed notion in our society that all ideas are equally valid and that truth is relative. Values are often culturally determined, but some things are more valuable than others. Some values have been held by all (or most) societies throughout history.

The first such value is truth, the subject of chapter 7. Societies have generally attached high value to truth and honesty over error and dishonesty. Truth is the basis for social order. Without truth, there can be no trust, and trust is what cements human relationships. Trust must be given and received.

The second value is goodness. History often divides the good guys from the bad. In old Westerns, it's pretty easy to tell them apart: Good guys wear white hats; bad guys wear black. In real life, no one is completely good or absolutely bad, but societies nevertheless agree that there is a difference between good and bad, right and wrong. In chapter 8, we consider who gets to decide which is which. Without an objective source of truth, good and bad are easily confused.

The final value we examine is beauty. Our cultural biases make it tricky to deal with the concept of beauty, but people throughout time have considered nature to be beautiful. Likewise, people have always regarded destruction as ugly. We believe that nature is beautiful because it is a reflection of God's nature. God is creative, so we reflect the image of God (the *imago Dei)* when we are creative. Satan is destructive, and thus destruction manifests our fallenness.

Part 4 deals with our actions. Our children may not care much about what we say, but they are watching what we do. Biblically speaking, certain behaviors and activities validate our faith in God. Without evidence of life change, however, our faith will be shallow and ineffective. It won't be the attractive force that our children need if they are going to grow deep in their relationship with God.

God calls us to make a difference for him in the world. In this section, we'll see how *faith* prompts us to engage the world, *hope* sustains us in our engagement, and *love* is the means by which we engage.

In chapter 10, we consider the life of William Wilberforce, who sparked the beginnings of the worldwide outlawing of human slavery. Wilberforce demonstrated that we can make a difference for social good if we allow God to change our hearts. We must tackle social issues as ambassadors of Christ. Real faith is never relegated to Sundays only. It permeates every part of our lives.

Chapter 11 is about the hope that is necessary for sustaining life. The question is not, do you have hope? but rather, in what are you placing your hope? Martin Luther King Jr. had the certain hope that he would inherit everlasting life with God, that justice would one day prevail, and that all our questions would be answered. These beliefs sustained his tireless efforts to see God's will accomplished in his generation. Such hope can be ours as well, and we can transfer it to our children by reminding them of great men and women of God.

Chapter 12 is about love, the core of the Christian life. As Christians, we are called to love our neighbors as ourselves; to care for marginalized people; to be Good Samaritans; and to feed the hungry, clothe the naked, and visit the sick and imprisoned. Nineteenth-century prison reformer Elizabeth Fry is a great example of someone who carried out these loving acts. Her compassion and compulsion to care for others came from her belief that every person has inherent value and dignity because they are created in God's image. Without that, we have no logical reason to care for others. When we treat people with love, we offer the best argument for the love and goodness of God, and we show our children what it looks like to be an ambassador for him.

Our conclusion suggests that you—yes, you!—will be able to pull this whole project off. As we've already said, parenting is difficult, but God has promised to give us the tools and resources we need to pass our faith along to the next generation. With God's help, by using the Bible and relying on the Holy Spirit, Christians can become better parents than they ever thought they could be.

Externals or Internals?

Jeff Sandstrom survived his childhood camp experience and became not only a good man but also a godly man. But like so many of us, he was a product of a system that defined success improperly. Success was often measured by what we externalized, not by what we internalized. When Jeff stood before his peers and their parents to recite his memorized speeches, his mission was accomplished. Never mind that the words coming out of his mouth hadn't yet reached his heart.

Contrast Jeff's childhood experience with the story of another little boy: Stuart and Kelley Hall's son, Grant. Stuart shared this story with us so that we could share it with you.

It is a glorious day for any parent when their children reach the point where they can use the bathroom and not go in their pants. The earlier that happens, the better. That was our experience with all three of our kids. Stunning how such a necessity of everyday life can be celebrated like the Red Sox winning the World Series. Sobering how such an occasion can bring you to your knees.

My wife, Kelley, began to notice blood on the toilet paper after my five-year-old son used the bathroom. A visit to the doctor calmed our fears a bit as our pediatrician assured us that Grant just suffered from a slight case of hemorrhoids. Not exactly the coolest thing for a kid in kindergarten to deal with.

Only days after that visit, however, Grant stood up from the toilet and blood spilled on the floor. Needless to say, we freaked. We made an immediate appointment with a specialist. After examining Grant, the specialist sat us down and said there was a strong possibility of cancer. Kelley and I sat there in shock. Exploratory surgery was necessary as quickly as possible, and we scheduled it for the following week.

I couldn't sleep that night. I pored over the Scriptures, begging God to show me a promise that he would heal my little boy. I did not find that promise. As far as I can surmise, nowhere does God promise to heal us from sickness or disease. He tells us that he *can,* but he does not promise that he *will.* The verse that got my attention was Psalm 31:24. David says, "Be strong and take heart, all you who hope in the Lord."

I wrote that verse in big letters on a piece of paper and put it by the coffee pot. Kelley and I made it a part of our conversation and prayers. I shared that verse with Grant and helped him to memorize it.

Two days before his surgery, I picked him up early from school for his pre-op tests. When he walked out of class, big tears were streaming down his face. For the first time since the whole ordeal began, he said, "Daddy, I'm scared." I quickly referred to that verse. I wish you could have witnessed my brave little boy, trying to catch his breath, dry his tears, and repeat those words: "Be strong and take heart, all you who hope in the Lord." Then again, I'm glad you weren't there, or you would have seen me turn my back to him and begin to cry.

We had to be at the hospital very early in the morning on the day of the surgery. The nurses gave Grant the equivalent of "children's cocaine" to sedate him. He started hallucinating, seeing cows flying around the room, talking incoherently about stuff only God could understand. As they rolled him away for the surgery, he smiled as his mom, grandparents, and I kissed him and told him that we loved him. When we reached that point in the hallway where we could go no further with him, his nurses said that we had to leave. As I leaned down to kiss Grant one more time, I wiped away a huge tear from his cheek and heard him mumbling something unintelligible.

I bent closer and finally understood what he was saying. Over and over, Grant was whispering, "Be strong and take heart, all you who hope in the Lord."[3]

One little boy memorized Scripture to gain status and acceptance. The other little boy memorized Scripture to gain courage and strength. One little boy learned about God in order to get something. The other little boy learned about God and became a different person. Both little boys externalized the right things. Only one boy also internalized the right things.

Jeff Sandstrom grew out of his externalism into a good and godly man, but he had to unlearn some of the bad habits of his childhood in order to gain a better understanding of godliness. Grant Hall—who survived the surgery and today is a fine, healthy young man—knew from a young age that true righteousness comes from the inside out. Real godly behavior begins with what's going on in our children's hearts and minds.

part 1
The High Cost of Parenting

In this first section, we encourage you to recover the lost role of parenting. Parents have the primary responsibility for the lifelong process of their children's faith development. We hope to build confidence and awareness by showing you the most common stages of that development and how parents can be more involved in leading their children to spiritual maturity through Christlike teaching.

Chapter 1
Parenting in an Age of Specialization

Given the amount of information available today on every imaginable subject, it's no wonder that we live in an age of specialists. In nearly every field, areas of expertise are shrinking, and the impact is acutely felt by parents. We want our kids to be healthy, so we make sure they have a doctor. It's hard to find a good, old-fashioned general practitioner these days, so our children may well have age-appropriate, gender-specific pediatricians.

We want our kids to be intellectually advanced, so we choose the locations of our homes according to school district, and we grill the teachers to ensure that our little Einsteins will have the best environment possible for developing their minds. Long gone are the days of the one-room schoolhouse with one teacher who taught all the subjects. Now we want young, attractive, energetic, multilingual math teachers who come in for one hour a day to teach only math (in a young, attractive, energetic, multilingual sort of way). If we want our child to learn Spanish, we'll find a good private tutor in the suburbs.

We want our children to be athletic, so we enroll them in sports programs. God forbid that one kid in America should miss out on youth soccer! We find that coaches tend to concentrate on one sport. After all, what does basketball have to do with soccer? We enroll our children in piano, art, and ballet lessons so that they will be cultured and appreciate the arts. Of course, ballet lessons for a four-year-old are mainly an excuse to dress her up in a pretty outfit. There's nothing wrong with that.

We send our overscheduled, under-rested, stressed-out kids from person to person to ensure that they are having well-rounded childhoods.

Do they have an appropriate balance of physical, cultural, and academic activities? Are they growing up with all the advantages we never had? Is there a specialist whose help we have not sought—a time-management expert or a nutritionist? Is there someone who can teach our children the most beneficial way of playing in the backyard?

There's nothing wrong with specializing in a particular skill or with seeking the expertise of someone uniquely qualified in a given field. If we can afford to give our children a leg up, we should do what we can. After all, we want the best for them, and we can't do it all by ourselves. No one says we have to coach Little League or learn a foreign language in order to parent our kids.

But who is responsible for our children's worldview and their connection with God?

FIRST THINGS FIRST

The fundamental assertion of faith among the people of God in the Old Testament was "Hear, O Israel: The LORD our God, the LORD is one. Love the LORD your God with all your heart and with all your soul and with all your strength" (Deuteronomy 6:4-5). Every time the people recited these words, they renewed their covenant with God. It was a gentle reminder of their true identity and of the relationship they had with the One who gave them that identity.

The Israelites recited these words at least twice every day—when they woke up and when they went to sleep. These were the first words taught to a Hebrew child who was learning to talk, and they were often the last words spoken at death by Israelites who took their commitment to God seriously. The *Shema* (a Hebrew word for "hear" or "listen"), as it came to be called, was to be their first sentence and their last sentence— of each day and of their lives. Every Jewish person knew this portion of Scripture as the very core of what it meant to be a child of God's covenant love. Everything else was subordinate to this overarching principle: Love God with everything you have!

Moses told them, "These commandments that I give you today are to be upon your hearts. Impress them on your children. Talk about them when you sit at home and when you walk along the road, when you lie down and when you get up. Tie them as symbols on your hands and bind them on your foreheads. Write them on the doorframes of your houses and on your gates" (Deuteronomy 6:6-9).

THEY'RE YOUR KIDS

Who is responsible for making sure that our children develop spiritually? The Bible is pretty clear on this. Parents have the primary responsibility for teaching their children to know and respect God. Their worldview will flow from the foundational text of the Shema, so parents should make every effort to teach this principle to their children.

This isn't just an Old Testament concept—in the New Testament, the apostle Paul says the same thing: "Fathers, do not exasperate your children; instead, bring them up in the training and instruction of the Lord" (Ephesians 6:4). Clearly, children are meant to be raised by their parents.

As obvious as this seems, however, we seem to have gotten off track somehow. With school, tutors, Little League, and band practice, a parent is just one of many voices in a child's life. As we spend less time with our children, we lose confidence in our ability to parent. Society also contributes to this anxiety. We are told that the state can do a better job of educating children. Every magazine rack contains articles on how to be a better parent. Radio and television experts sometimes belittle traditional families with traditional values. In his book *You're a Better Parent Than You Think!* Dr. Ray Guarendi notes, "We are in the midst of a rush into child-raising awareness—a rush that is having an unexpected backlash on parents. It is breeding worry, guilt, indecision, and a host of other uncomfortable emotions that can undermine self-assured parenting."[1]

On the whole, we live in an increasingly self-consumed society that no longer prizes such values as sacrifice and selflessness. This has created a startling lack of heroism in our culture as fewer people are willing to set aside their personal comfort and safety for the good of others. It doesn't take much of this prevailing sentiment to persuade parents that they can continue to pursue their own interests with minimal interference from their children—provided that they allow other people to raise their children for them.

Society thus tells us that we are probably not very effective as parents and that we have our own things going and shouldn't have to give them up. These two ideas combine to generate some serious consequences. It has now become acceptable, even normative, for parents to abdicate their role as the primary guardians of their children.

Under such intense scrutiny and pressure, many parents are content to allow institutions and organizations to educate and socialize their children. Schools and private tutors are readily available for everything from horseback riding and computer skills to table manners. Unfortunately, many people assume that they can also outsource their children's spiritual development.

It is shocking that the church often contributes to this upside-down philosophy. All too often, churches and pastors are eager to ride in on white horses, saying, "Leave those kids to us; we'll take care of them! Just drop them off in our age-appropriate, self-esteem-building, sterilized children's ministry environments. We'll let you know when they're ready to be picked up."

It is sad that churches have also played on the selfish mentality of many parents by billing their children's ministry as child care. "Mom and Dad are free to build themselves up while we take care of their children." Very few churches offer meaningful intergenerational gatherings where parents and children can together learn the basics of faith and how to live it out at home.

Should we let the professionals take care of it? After all, you probably didn't go to seminary. You don't know Greek or Hebrew, and you may not even know all the books of the Bible. How can you be responsible for the faith development of your kids? When everything around us requires a specialist, how can we presume to be our children's spiritual mentors—when we don't even have things figured out for ourselves?

We have made the faith development of children church-based and home-supported. But look through the Bible sometime for even a single verse about how the church is supposed to raise children. You will find that the Bible repeatedly tells parents how to relate to their own kids. In other words, churches should be assisting parents as they work at home to train their children and instruct them in the knowledge of the Lord. There is a lot of truth to the old cliché "It takes a village to raise a child." But the village—the community of faith surrounding the family—must never replace parents as the primary caregivers, guardians, and instructors of children. Rather than eroding the confidence of parents or feeding their naturally selfish urges, churches should offer their resources and guidance to parents. They should avoid the trap of thinking that they are the primary source of spiritual development for children.

The Bible clearly says the primary responsibility for instilling faith and values in the next generation belongs to moms and dads who must commit time, effort, prayer, learning, and growth to this endeavor. We shouldn't expect it to be easy—and we cannot help our children grow in spiritual things if we are spiritually immature ourselves.

IS IT IN YOU?

Anyone who has ever flown with children knows the preflight statement, "In the case of an unexpected loss of cabin pressure, oxygen masks will drop from the panel above you. Those traveling with small children should secure their own mask before attempting to assist others."[2]

Most parents think that it would be far more appropriate to make sure that the kids are okay first, but the airlines have a good reason for this policy. Parents are oxygen-givers. Our children—especially if they are young—depend on us for nearly everything. If a parent passes out, the kids are in trouble! Children need parents who are clearheaded and alert. You have to take care of yourself first when others are counting on you.

That's why Moses says, "These commandments that I give you today are to be upon your hearts" *before* he says, "Impress them on your children." It's impossible to give something away if you don't have it. Otherwise you can only fake it, and children are very good at detecting phoniness. Children look to their parents for ideas on how to live their faith. If parents aren't providing an example of what faith looks like in the rough-and-tumble of everyday life, children cannot be expected to "do as I say and not as I do."

As parents, we find time for the things that matter most. We manage to eat, bathe, and sleep—most days at least (unless we have a two-year-old, and then all bets are off). Most of us even find time to exercise and keep ourselves physically fit. Yet we claim not to have enough time to maintain our connection with God.

In the opening chapter of his book *Finding God in Unexpected Places,* Philip Yancey analyzes America's health craze and its obsession with physical fitness. Yancey, an avid runner, joined a Chicago health club after a foot injury prevented him from running. After his experiences at the health club, he wrote:

> In the end, the health club stands as a pagan temple. Its members strive to preserve only one part of the person: the body, which is the least enduring part of all. . . . Physical training is of some value, Paul advised Timothy, but godliness has value for all things, holding promise for both the present life and the life to come (1 Timothy 4:8). As I pedaled, straining against computer-generated hills, I had to ask myself: What is my spiritual counterpart to the Chicago Health Club? And then, more troubling: How much time and energy do I devote to each?[3]

We need exercise. We are, after all, stewards of life and health just as we are stewards of money and talents. But we must place first things first.

THE HIGH STAKES OF PARENTING

A human being enters the world bearing an immortal soul. Every child will one day give an account of his or her life to a holy judge. All of us will face an unending eternity of either unspeakable joy or unbearable separation from God. In our society, parents are expected to think a lot about how to give their children temporal gifts—a nice house, good vacations, the best education—but these same parents neglect the one gift that will last for eternity. Parents love their children best by preparing them to stand before God.

Moses gave the Israelites clear instructions on helping their children to develop a relationship with their Creator. He warned the people about the dangers of departing from God's ways. "Do not follow other gods, the gods of the peoples around you; for the LORD your God, who is among you, is a jealous God and his anger will burn against you, and he will destroy you from the face of the land. Do not test the LORD your God" (Deuteronomy 6:14-16).

How did the Israelites respond to this clear warning? Apparently they did quite well—for a generation. Joshua inherited the position of leadership from Moses and lived to be 110 years old.[4] During his lifetime, he brought the Israelites into the Promised Land, led them to many victories, and set a great example of a life of faith. After his death, others of his generation lived on for a while, but eventually they died as well. "The people served the LORD throughout the lifetime of Joshua and of the elders who outlived him and who had seen all the great things the LORD had done for Israel" (Judges 2:7). While the memory of God's greatness and the work he did for Israel was alive, the people maintained their devotion to God.

After the death of Joshua and those who had seen God's mighty acts, "another generation grew up, who knew neither the LORD nor what he had done for Israel. Then the Israelites did evil in the eyes of the LORD and served the Baals" (Judges 2:10-11). Therefore, "in his anger against Israel the LORD handed them over to raiders who plundered them. He sold them to their enemies all around, whom they were no longer able to resist" (Judges 2:14).

The people honored God because Joshua and his generation had direct personal knowledge of God's mighty acts among the people. The next generation didn't know God or his work on their behalf. This new generation turned to other gods, and the true God brought judgment upon them.

Judges is perhaps the saddest book in the Bible. It follows the children of Israel during one of the darkest times in their history and traces a depressing cycle: The Israelites honor God; the Israelites forget God; the Israelites are enslaved; the Israelites call out to God; God raises up a judge; the Israelites are delivered. Then the process is repeated—six times! If only the people had taken Moses' instructions from Deuteronomy 6 seriously, the whole pattern could have been avoided. Every time the cycle came back around to the part where they were delivered and again honored God, they had a chance to avoid repeating the process. And every time, the parents failed to pass the lessons they had learned on to their children.

If only this historical message no longer applied to God's people! Unfortunately, the cycle continues. Each time a baby is born, the parents have a choice: Will we pass the torch of faith to this child, or will we allow the darkness to claim another generation? Unless we parents teach our children about God and pass on a Christian worldview to them, the problems of our society will continue. We can turn the tide if we will courageously take back the responsibility that has been ours all along.

Chapter 2
Faith Development

A tree is a tree is a tree, but what separates a sapling from a towering oak? Generally speaking, a newly planted tree can be uprooted rather easily, whereas an older tree can often withstand hurricane-force winds. The difference is not in the size or the kind of tree, but in the tree's maturity. Trees grow stronger over time as they become more deeply and firmly rooted in the soil. We would be surprised to find a tree growing smaller and less able to bear the onslaught of wind and rain as the years progressed.

Even if we're not dendrochronologists, we know that most trees develop according to an expected pattern, adding rings for every year of their existence. When a tree dies, it stops growing.

Our faith also has an expected pattern of growth and development. As long as our faith is alive, it should be adding layers and putting down roots, becoming stronger and better able to withstand the pressures and difficulties of life. We don't have a static, one-size-fits-all faith that we are handed on the day we accept Jesus as our rescuer and leader.

Our faith is a seed that God plants in our lives, and as we grow through various stages, our faith becomes stronger. As our faith grows from infancy to adulthood, there is no shortcut to spiritual maturity. As with any other growth process, we must begin at the beginning and proceed through the middle if we hope for our character to be transformed in a way that honors Jesus now and to the end. If a person's faith is not allowed to go through all the necessary stages, it may become stunted or even be aborted.

STAGES OF FAITH

Human beings are born into the world with immortal souls, and every child will eventually stand before a holy and just God to give an account of his or her life. As difficult as this is for parents to realize, our children will one day face an eternal destiny of unspeakable joy or unbearable separation from God. Therefore, it is extremely important for us as parents to take responsibility for shaping our children's worldview. Our children must decide for themselves whether they will follow Christ, but we can nudge them in that direction.

Parents in our society think long and hard about how to give their children the best this world has to offer. We seek wise counsel regarding where to live, what the educational options are, where we will vacation, and what kinds of activities our kids should be involved in. We shuttle them back and forth from lessons and field trips, and we help them navigate extracurricular obstacle courses that will get them into the best universities. We often forget that four hundred years from now, their college degree will be less important than a personal relationship with their Creator.

In *Bringing Up Children in the Christian Faith,* John H. Westerhoff has written about faith development in children. Using very broad strokes, he has discerned four distinct stages of faith. The first stage, "experiential faith," is gained from interaction with significant others who are people of faith. The apostle Paul writes of his young companion Timothy that his faith was nurtured by his mother, Eunice, and his grandmother, Lois. Infants raised in Christian homes have a relationship with God because a lifestyle of faith is all they have ever known, and the significant people in their lives are Christians. People in this stage believe primarily because it's all they have ever experienced.

The second stage is "affiliative faith," which grows through involvement in a faith community. It comes by sharing in the worship, ministry, decision making, and caring life of the church. Paul first encountered Timothy when he visited Lystra, where Timothy was highly regarded as a member of the community. Children whose parents include them in church-related activities have a relationship with God because all of the people around them have a relationship with God. People in this stage believe primarily because they belong to a group of people who believe.

The third stage is "inquisitive faith." This questioning phase usually occurs sometime in adolescence for children raised in Christian homes. Paul took Timothy on one of his missionary journeys. As Timothy participated in Paul's mission, asked questions, and tested his gifts, his faith was challenged and strengthened. This is the stage that most Christian parents fear and that some churches and families discourage altogether. However, if a young person does not fully experience this stage, his or her faith development will be compromised.

The fourth stage is "owned faith." This is a faith that has developed and has been tested. At this stage, people are committed to certain beliefs, attitudes, and practices that they have chosen for themselves. Unless people are allowed to proceed through the inquisitive stage, they will not be personally invested in their beliefs. At this last stage, a person believes because his or her faith has withstood the crucible moments of life, and he or she is in a position to help others. Timothy was sent to resolve problems in Corinth; then he became a leader of the church in Ephesus.

These stages may be recycled a few times during a person's life, as new questions and challenges emerge and are resolved through further growth. However, mature Christians do not rely solely on the beliefs of others as the basis for their faith. Their faith has been tested, and they have made it their own. Christians continue to rely on the nurture, guidance, and encouragement of other Christians, but just as children outgrow their total dependence on their parents for physical nurture and support, mature Christians are able to maintain their faith even when people around them exhibit differing beliefs and lifestyles.

As parents, we want more than anything for our children to own their faith. We want them to love God and to serve, enjoy, trust, and partner with him because they want to, not because of who their parents are or because they're in a church where that's expected. We want them to do these things because they have made the choice to do so from the core of their own souls.

Parents cannot make this happen. We live as if there were a hard-and-fast, cause-and-effect law at work guaranteeing that if we do certain things, our children will own their faith. We expect there to be a magical formula for raising children that will ensure their eternal destiny, like Francis Schaeffer's image of God as a cosmic vending machine. *But this is not the case.* Most Christians have probably read or heard Proverbs 22:6, which says, "Train a child in the way he should go, and when he is old he will not turn from it." Entire books have been written based on this verse, giving parents "no fail" solutions to getting their kids to behave. But we must remember that proverbs are descriptions of the way life usually works; they're *not* promises. Every human being is born with a will of his or her own. That free will entails the ability and the responsibility to choose a life path. The more we manipulate our children's choices (and however well-intentioned we may be in doing so), the more we will damage their faith development.

The tragic story of Todd Marinovich is widely known in sports circles. Todd's father, Marv, was a co-captain for the 1962 national champions, the University of Southern California Trojans, and an offensive lineman and assistant coach for the Oakland Raiders. He decided that his son would have the perfect football upbringing. Todd was never allowed to eat sugar or fast food or watch cartoons. Instead of playmates, Todd had a nutritionist and a personal trainer. By age ten, Todd had a professional throwing coach grooming him to be a quarterback. Marv chose Todd's middle school and high school based on their football programs. Everything seemed to be working according to plan when *USA Today* named Todd the 1987 high school player of the year.

Todd went to USC and led the Trojans to a Rose Bowl victory as a redshirt freshman, but he was unaccustomed to freedom. Out from under the watchful eye of his domineering and overprotective father, Todd began to experiment—first with McDonald's, and then with marijuana. He was drafted by the Raiders, by then in Los Angeles, and started as a rookie. But he lasted only two years before imploding, both personally and professionally. Drug problems contributed to the end of his NFL career, and he was arrested on drug charges several times, including as recently as May 2005. After leaving the Raiders, he played briefly in the Canadian Football League and the Arena Football League, but was out of professional football altogether by 2001. After his arrest in 2005, he listed his occupation as "unemployed artist."[1]

Todd is accountable for his poor choices, but his father initiated the damage by manipulating Todd and failing to teach him how to make his own good decisions about how to live.

There are things we can do as parents to alter the trajectory of our children's lives—to nudge them in the direction of God or to alienate them from him. If it is important to us that our children have a mature faith, we should understand the four stages of faith development and realize that our children must pass through each of the first three in order to get to the fourth. These stages are not always neatly divided and their boundaries are often fuzzy, but this template can help us to be aware of which stage our child is in and to anticipate what lies ahead.

The Experiential Stage

When children are very young, they may not be able to understand the fine points of doctrine, but they sometimes demonstrate openness to God's work in their lives that far surpasses that of adults. We often underestimate their awareness of God's presence and activity.

In *The Religious Potential of the Child,* Sofia Cavalletti discusses spirituality in young children—specifically those between the ages of three and six. She has observed that children don't really need adult role models in order to connect meaningfully with God, though knowing spiritually minded adults can be a positive experience for them. Children can and often do connect with God on their own—something Cavalletti refers to as "spontaneous religiousness."[2] As children get older, this connection is more likely to come as a logical deduction. For example, a child may understand that because nothing comes from nothing, life must not have been formed by chance but must have emerged from an eternal source.

This kind of connection, however, can only come after a child has learned to think in the abstract—after the age of seven or so.

Cavalletti also cites some examples of younger children connecting with God in a way that is "more deeply rooted than in the intellect alone." One such example involves a three-year-old girl who was raised "without the slightest religious influence."[3]

> The child did not go to nursery school; no one at home . . . had ever spoken of God; the child had never gone to church. One day she questioned her father about the origin of the world: "Where does the world come from?" Her father replied, in a manner consistent with his ideas, with a discourse that was materialistic in nature; then he added: "However, there are those who say that all this comes from a very powerful being, and they call him God." At this point, the little girl began to run like a whirlwind around the room in a burst of joy, and exclaimed: "I knew what you told me wasn't true; it is Him, it is Him!"[4]

Another educator, Edward Robinson, gathered more than four thousand first-person accounts of childhood religious experiences as recollected by adults later in life. His research shows that "children can and do have profound, mature religious experiences, which can only in later life be named, described, explained, or comprehended." In short, "we hear God speak before we can express what God says."[5]

One of the accounts that Robinson relates is from a man simply known as "M":

> The circumstances were: dusk, summertime, and I one of a crowd of grown-ups and children assembled round the shore of a large ornamental lake, waiting for full darkness before a firework display was to begin. A breeze stirred the leaves of a group of poplars just to my right; stirred, they gave a fluttering sound. There, then, I knew or felt or experienced—what? Incommunicable now, but then much more so. The sensations were of awe or wonder,

and a sense of astounding beauty—at that moment in dusk—and the perception that *it* would have gone when it was dark and the fireworks began. And so it was.[6]

Later, Robinson met M and talked about that experience. Here is an excerpt of what M had to say about it:

> It's very difficult to say that it revealed—what? The existence of infinity? The fact of divinity? I wouldn't have had the language at my command as a child to formulate such things, so that if I speak about it now it is with the language and ideas of a mature person. But from my present age, looking back some half a century, I would say that I did then experience—what? A truth, a fact, the existence of the divine. What happened was telling me something. But what was it telling? The fact of divinity, that it was good? Not so much the moral sense, but that it was beautiful, yes, sacred.[7]

The Bible often talks about God speaking to children, such as Samuel or Josiah. In the New Testament, little children are magnetically drawn to Jesus. Just as children are born with an innate capacity to walk or speak, they are born with an innate capacity to relate to God, and this ability may be stronger than any of their other instincts. When they are in this early stage of development, parents can provide an environment rich in opportunities for their kids to hear God's story and experience its reality. This will take many different forms, given the unique makeup of each family, but it should probably include making the Bible available to children and encouraging them to communicate openly and honestly with God. Bob Russell, the former senior minister of Southeast Christian Church in Louisville, Kentucky, shares this story about one of his sons:

> From the time that our children were little, we have had prayer and read a Bible story to them when they went to bed each night. The prayers started out as "Now I lay me down to sleep" and eventually graduated to their saying their own. To be honest, that

prayer time was usually very perfunctory, and sometimes my boys would even mix up "Now I lay me down to sleep" with "God is great; God is good." I wondered, at times, if I was accomplishing anything. But slowly they learned the Bible, and those perfunctory prayers sank in, even though they weren't dramatic.

When one of my sons was in his teenage years, we discovered that he had violated a family principle, and he was in trouble—big time. I confronted him on the issue, and he admitted that he had broken the rule. Immediately he broke into tears and apologized.

I was still pretty angry and didn't respond very warmly to him. He sobbed and said, "Dad, could we pray or something?" That broke my heart. As we knelt at the couch, put our arms around each other, and prayed, I felt closer to my son than I had for an awfully long time.

His open confession of wrongdoing and his recognition of the necessity for rules were important. It was equally important that he wanted to pray and ask for God's forgiveness. If it had not been for those perfunctory prayers together in childhood, I really doubt that this would have been his response when he needed God's forgiveness and my forgiveness.

We don't communicate our values and worldview by sitting down and giving a lecture for an hour, passing along a book, or listening to a sermon. We must pray with our children as well as for them. Our responsibility as parents is to teach our children—through example and participation—what it is to worship God on a daily basis.[8]

It is important to teach young children that they can talk directly to God and that they can share whatever is on their mind without using big words or a certain tone of voice. As Bob said, some days it will seem that you are just going through the motions, but gradually they will learn, it will become a habit, and prayer will be their first recourse in difficult times.

It is appropriate to suit the length and complexity of your prayers to the receptivity of your child. For example, it is probably unrealistic to expect a three-year-old to sit still while you read Psalm 119 and pray through your church's sick list. On the other hand, a nine-year-old is probably a little beyond "Now I lay me down to sleep." Praying with your children does not need to be formal. Keeping it simple can help children learn that God isn't interested in technicalities. He's interested in us just as we are. We can talk to God with our children at any time—when we see beauty in nature, when we sit down to eat, when we receive a gift. If you cultivate a prayerful environment in your home, children will see prayer as a normal part of everyday life.

Bob says, "We must pray *with* our children as well as *for* them." He assumes that we will be praying for our children and that most parents would agree with this. I know that some parents might not pray at all if it were not for their children—kids have a way of driving the most even-tempered parents to their knees. But how do we pray for them, and what should we pray for? Should we ask God to protect our children from every hardship? Should we ask God to make them do the right things? Parents must wrestle with these hard questions.

In *How Would Jesus Raise a Child?* Dr. Teresa Whitehurst observes that the Christian community has largely failed to apply the teachings and example of Jesus in the parenting realm, claiming that because he was not a parent, he has nothing relevant to say on the topic. Of course, Jesus never ran a business, led a church, or got married, yet we regularly apply his teachings in these realms. Her point is valid—we should ask ourselves how Jesus would raise our children and give particular attention to how Jesus might pray for them.

On the night before he was betrayed, Jesus told Peter, "Satan is going to tempt you as you've never been tempted before. But I'm praying for you. After it's all over, remember to come back and strengthen every-one else, okay?" (Luke 22:31-32, our paraphrase). It's interesting that Jesus didn't try to fix Peter, give advice, or lecture him. Neither did he protect Peter from the trial he was about to face. He just prayed for Peter and told him that he was doing so.

At his moment of deepest concern, Jesus knew that the single most powerful way to benefit a person whom he loved deeply was to pray for him. Very often we want to control our kids or manipulate their circumstances, and we ask God to help us do this. However, in God's design, things don't work that way. Even young children in the first stage of faith development will defy attempts to control and manipulate them. Your tactics may seem effective in modifying your child's behavior—in the short term. In the long run, your child will resent your micromanagement and will likely rebel against it.

This can be incredibly frustrating to live through, but in the long term it is liberating. If we were allowed too much control over our children, we would inevitably damage them, stunt their development, and hinder them from cultivating healthy relationships with God, others, and themselves. Our wise God has established patterns of growth and maturity that we would be wise not to ignore. The single most powerful thing you can do for your kids is to pray for them. You need not have a perfect faith in order to do this, but perhaps the second most powerful thing you can do for your kids is whatever it takes to keep yourself spiritually healthy.

At this stage, children love stories, and it is appropriate to give them consistent exposure to the Bible. Remember, however, that children may have profound experiences with God without being able to explain them in words. Children can benefit greatly from hearing Bible stories without your having to unpack all of their theological implications. Also, although we believe that every story in the Bible is equally inspired, every story is not equally important, relevant, or appropriate to every stage of your child's life. Some stories apply more significantly and directly to a young child's world than others. The moral complexities surrounding the destruction of Sodom are less important for kids in the experiential stage of faith development than during their inquisitive stage. The story of Joseph and Potiphar's wife will be more relevant to a teenager than to a six-year-old.

Be tenacious and rigorous about involving your kids in a community of faith. At the very least, this will mean taking your kids to church on a regular basis. Some churches partner with parents by supplying them with resources for instilling faith principles and godly character in children. Perhaps you will need to rearrange some things in your schedule, but the rewards will far outweigh any sacrifices you make. Your children will benefit from knowing other adults and children who say and believe the same things as their parents. This will be especially helpful as they transition from the first stage to the second.

The Affiliative Stage

It is sad but true that at a certain age your kids will no longer believe that you are the smartest and most powerful being in the universe. This is actually a good experience . . . for them. But it can be a crushing blow to parental egos, especially if we have bought into the myth that we can control our children and protect them from every big bad wolf on the block.

Sometime around the ages of ten to twelve, kids begin to realize that parents cannot be everywhere or protect them from everything. They may even begin to notice that we don't know everything or have it all together. At this time they are usually also experiencing a profound longing to connect with and belong to other people, primarily their own peers. Relationships take on a much greater significance as children learn the basic skills of building strong and stable social networks.

During this stage kids desperately want to be part of something bigger than themselves. They want to be part of a community, and they want to be independently and directly connected with something transcendent. By this time we hope that our children have found this kind of support system in a faith-based environment. We then pray that our transcendent God will draw their hearts into a personally meaningful connection.

Jean Piaget, a Swiss researcher who specializes in how we construct our views of reality, reminds us that at this stage of childhood development, "it is more important for children to be incorporated into a loving community than to be given abstractions about God's love."[9]

When these supports are absent, children who are not involved in a church community that meets their relational needs can fall prey to cults or gangs, and they will be very susceptible to the typical clique mentality at school. These groups attract preteens and adolescents because they offer a sense of "pseudobelonging." They offer acceptance, structure, motivation, accountability, protection, approval, and empowerment. These essential things should be provided in the home and church settings.

Parents can and should help their children to connect with others in meaningful ways. The church and the home should be the primary locations where these connections are made and maintained. This will mean helping our children to select friends wisely, getting to know our children's friends, and doing everything possible to make our homes available and attractive. Lanny Donoho, president and creative director of BigStuf, Inc., decided to take this seriously when his oldest son was sixteen. Here's his story:

> When my firstborn son reached sixteen in such a short period of time, I realized that he had already lived in my house eight times longer than he would be staying. In other words, he might only be living full-time here for two more years. That was sobering, to say the least. Now that he was driving, he had friends who lived across town, and every weekend he wanted to head to their houses and even spend the night.
>
> Separation anxiety isn't just for two-year-olds; it's also for parents of teenagers. Even though I'd been in youth ministry, I couldn't figure out why my son wanted to hang out over there instead of staying home with his dear old dad. Well . . . maybe I could figure it out, but I just didn't want to.
>
> One Friday night, a situation helped me to develop a plan to defer my separation anxiety for a while. My son was gone, supposedly to his friend's house, and he was supposed to be home by 9:30 p.m.
>
> When curfew came and went, we began to worry a bit. At 10:00, we called him on his cell phone, but he didn't answer. We then realized, to our horror, that we really didn't know the names

of his friends or who we could call to see if he was at another friend's house. By 10:30, we were randomly calling familiar-sounding names out of his high school directory.

At 11:00, I decided to try my skill at navigating a large neighborhood across town, trusting that my memory of having delivered him there once long ago would kick into gear and I could find the house where he was supposed to be.

At 11:30 p.m., I found a house that looked familiar. His car was in the driveway, so I figured this must be the place. I knocked. No one answered. I tried the door, and it opened. Five hundred decibels of noise were blaring from the basement, so I headed downstairs hoping that I would find him all in one piece. There he was, bouncing around on his friend's Dance Dance Revolution pad and having the time of his life.

I didn't say a word as I grabbed him by the collar and forced him up the stairs so he could follow me home.

Time gets away from teenagers. They can't hear phones when the sound system and video games are pounding, and they tend to forget that someone may be home wondering if they're alive.

I was angry, frustrated, and scared to death for a while, but something good came out of that night. I now have a new kind of basement. We have a Dance Dance Revolution pad and something that will crank up to about five hundred decibels. We have a big-screen TV, so movies look great. There's a microwave and a fridge with food in it. The Nintendo and Xbox are hooked up, and there are lots of comfy places to sit and lie around. All the kids want to hang out at my house now.

I've got two more years with my son, and then I have two younger guys coming right up. If they're going to hang out with their friends, I'm not going to force them to come here. But I'm going to do my best to make our house the place where they want to be. Then maybe I won't have to drive around scouting out houses at 11:30 p.m. anymore.[10]

Lanny spent a lot of money on his basement, but he sees it as an investment. It may not appear profitable in the short term, but it should pay huge dividends in the future.

Some parents don't want their kids' friends hanging out at their house. We're not saying that this is easy. Any parent who has ever been through the experience knows that the one thing children won't do at a sleepover is actually sleep. Children and their friends tend to be hard on furniture. They may not understand the dinstinctions of "good china" or "guest towels." But all of those things are just that: things. Things don't last forever—the soul of your child will. In the affiliative stage of faith, the people your children hang out with are very important. You need to know them, so make every effort to welcome them into your home.

This is also a good time to introduce your children to people who are different from themselves in socioeconomics, ethnicity, and opportunities. It is an excellent time to help your kids learn to serve. Otherwise the prevailing culture will turn them into mall rats. Children at this stage of development often have a desire to serve, give, and make a difference in their world, and they are often told that they will have to wait until they're older to do something meaningful. Help them to become part of a serving community—volunteering at a soup kitchen or some benevolent program at church or in the community—to dispel the idea that they are helpless in the face of poverty and injustice.

As your kids grow older, they need to hear their parents speak directly about faith and spiritual growth. One impressive thing that parents can do is to tell their children their own faith story. Talk to your kids about your life with God. Tell them how and why you became a Christian. Tell them about times when you've blown it and God has shown you mercy. Tell them about times when God has prompted you to do something and you've done it. Tell them about your doubts, because they will doubt, and they need to know it is normal.

Many parents avoid doing this because they think that their own lives have to be perfect or that they have to know all the answers before they can minister to their children. Don't be unrealistic—that time is never going to come. Start talking to your children about the things that matter most. Talk about music, books, nature, beauty, art, stars, and animals, and point your kids to the Creator behind them. Help your children to establish the habit of paying attention to the world and of looking behind what they see.

The Inquisitive Stage

Parents don't want their children to remain children forever. This might seem to simplify life, but it would be a cruel thing to wish on our kids. They were born to grow up into mature, responsible adults who will contribute to the Kingdom of God. All parents want their children to grow, thrive, and flourish—physically, emotionally, and especially spiritually.

We want our children to possess a strong, personal faith that they can live by, witness to, and even be willing to die for. We don't want them to believe simply because they have Christian parents or because all of the people around them believe. We want them to believe because they have made a decision to do so from the core of their being. We want their faith to be theirs—or at least we think we do.

In order for our children to get to that desired fourth level of faith, they have to go through the third level—the inquisitive stage. This can be a struggle for both parents and kids. Usually sometime in adolescence children begin asking questions such as, "How do we really know the Christian faith is the right one?" or "How do we know there really is a God?" or "If God is so powerful and so loving, why do bad things happen to good people?" You know—the kinds of questions we're all prepared to answer and gladly welcome. Yeah, right!

Unfortunately, in many churches and homes these questions are not encouraged. Rather, those who ask such questions are shunned and treated like social misfits. Some churches and homes foster a culture of fear in which actively seeking answers to difficult questions is viewed as disloyal and those who dare to doubt are swiftly punished. Perhaps this is one explanation for the ridiculously high dropout rate among teenagers in evangelical churches.

We cannot keep our kids from entering the inquisitive stage. We can prepare them for it and walk through it with them, but we cannot prevent it. There are only three exits from the inquisitive stage. Children can move on to the next stage of faith; their faith can regress and become stunted; or their faith can be aborted altogether. As children go through the inquisitive stage of faith development, the questions they will raise are difficult for even trained theologians to answer. How are parents supposed to deal with the complex issues raised by their children's questions?

We don't have to pretend that there are easy answers or that we know them all. Our kids will see through our bluff in any case. It's okay to say, "I haven't got everything figured out, and I still have some questions myself." The good news is that we have a faith—and a God—that hold up very well under scrutiny. God has never been afraid of our questions, and we don't need to be afraid of what our children will ask us.

Often the best thing we can do for our children is simply to provide a safe place and a safe person with whom they can raise these questions. If we could answer all of their questions for them, their faith still wouldn't be their own. They need to work and investigate, but we needn't be completely hands-off during this process either. At this phase it is critical for parents to use every resource available to them—music, movies, books, concerts. Get a copy of a book such as *The Case for Christ* by Lee Strobel, and read it together with your child. Once a week or so, take him or her out for a treat and talk about a chapter from the book. Many such books are now packaged in versions specifically for teenagers. Take your children to the park and ask them about sunsets or the laws of physics. Ask your kids about the lyrics to the music they're listening to and the content of the movies they watch. This doesn't have to be a scary, formal thing. It can be an adventure that bonds you with your teenager.

One of the smartest things you can do for your children is to plan for them to talk about things with someone other than you. There comes a time in every child's life when, for some inexplicable reason, they just don't want to share everything with Mom or Dad. What is worse is that you're likely to hear, at least once during your child's adolescence, something you've said a hundred times that has gone completely ignored until a coach or a teacher says the exact same thing. Now all of a sudden it makes perfect sense to your kid.

As a parent, you have two choices when faced with this reality. You can scream, "I've said that a hundred times! Why haven't you ever listened to me?" (If you take this route, be prepared for a blank stare and the question "When did you say that?") Or you can embrace this and be proactive. You can provide your child with environments where other responsible adults (people who believe and say the same kinds of things you believe and say) will invest in your child's life. You may need to leave your current church in order to find one that will partner with you in this endeavor, but the stakes are high enough to justify that.

Whatever you do or don't do as a parent, whatever else you work hard for to give your children, don't neglect their souls. Help them through these early stages of faith so that they can grow to have a faith of their own. The process may be difficult at times, especially during the inquisitive phase, but it can also be fun. One of the great things about kids is that they make us look at faith in fresh ways. You can help your kids grow closer to God, but your kids can help *you* just as much.

Parenting is a launching process. This is a good thing, but we are sometimes sad when we think about the day our children will move out into the world. More significantly, a day is coming when our children will face a holy and just God. The thought of missing one child through all eternity is unendurable. Talk to your kids about your faith and pray for them so that when the last day comes, you will be ready, and so will they!

The Owned Stage

We want for our kids to arrive at the stage of "owned faith," a place where they own their faith, and their faith owns them. When children own their faith, they commit themselves to a lifestyle and behavior that is consistent with what they believe. An owned faith is self-directed, not a reaction to anyone (parents, peers) or anything (cultural pressures) else.

Children who own their faith do not need everyone else to believe what they believe. They are able to tolerate the views of others without compromising their own faith.

It is important to note that having an owned faith does not mean that all doubts and questions are gone forever. There may be times when a person goes from the owned stage back into the inquisitive stage. But someone who owns his or her faith has internalized it to some significant degree, and an authentic relationship with God is in the works. Faith development is a lifelong process that will never be completed this side of eternity, but an owned faith is a benchmark of spiritual maturity.

There's an old story about a rabbi and his servant. The rabbi was very well known and traveled from place to place delivering an exceptionally stirring speech on the purpose of the Law. The rabbi's servant always traveled with him but was often overlooked and treated with disdain by those who came to hear the great expert.

One day as they were on their way to another lecture, the rabbi said to the servant, "Sometimes I get tired of going all over creation delivering the same message over and over again. I feel that if I have to give this lecture one more time, I'll fall asleep in the middle of it."

The servant responded, "I know what you mean. I've been with you every time you've given it. I could probably recite it word for word by now."

The rabbi perked up at this and said, "Well, why don't you? Let's switch places for this one. You pretend to be the rabbi, and I'll pretend to be the servant."

The servant was nervous at the thought, but he reasoned that it might give the rabbi a better idea of what a servant had to endure. He also thought it might be nice to be treated with respect and admiration.

They switched clothes, and the ruse began. The rabbi was overlooked and treated with disdain while the servant was treated like royalty. The servant delivered the lecture flawlessly—even answering a few tricky questions with surprising insight. As the event drew to a close, the servant, feeling very proud of himself, said to the audience, "I have time for one more question, and then my servant and I must be going."

A man asked an extremely esoteric question about some ambiguous point of the Law, digressing here and there to let everyone in the audience know how learned he was. When he finished, the servant fixed the man with a steely gaze and said, "Is that the hardest question you can think of? The answer to that question is so simple that I'll have my servant come up and explain it to you."

THE DANGERS OF BEING SMART

Sometimes smart people feel that they have to work very hard to let everyone else know just how smart they are. Intelligence does not always breed security and self-assurance. It is part of our fallen nature to compete for status and importance. When we are insecure in our identity as children of God, we waste time and energy trying to manage other people's impressions of us. We spin things and manipulate the truth—ultimately at our own expense—because we so desperately want others to think highly of us.

If we can't get our peers to believe that we're better, smarter, and more together than we really are, we often settle for fooling our kids. After all, they're naive and impressionable. When they first arrive on the scene, they are completely dependent upon us. It's almost inevitable that we will seem like gods to our children, so why not promote that idea a little and boost our fragile egos while we're at it?

This undermines our personal growth. We will never develop into the mature people God wants us to be until we rest in the security that comes from him alone. While we are busy investing in image maintenance, our attempts to connect deeply with God will be unsatisfactory and we will find it difficult to guide our children in their search for God. Insisting that our children view us as superiors is not godly behavior. God may occasionally challenge his servants to a contest ("Job, I have a few questions for you. . . ."), but that is the exception to the rule. Generally, if people want to believe that they are smarter than God, God will allow them enough rope to hang themselves.

God is not indifferent to us or unwilling to intervene to protect us from ourselves, but as C. S. Lewis said, "There are only two kinds of people in the end: those who say to God, 'Thy will be done,' and those to whom God says . . . '*Thy* will be done.'"[1] God doesn't need to flex his muscles; he prefers it when people obey him willingly.

JESUS THE TEACHER

In the last century, an academic debate to the effect that Jesus of Nazareth was no more than an incredible teacher spilled over into everyday discussions. One side of the debate claimed that though Jesus said many important and wise things, he was just a person. The other side said, "No, Jesus was more than that. He was a man, but he was also deity. The Jesus of history is also the Son of God."

We believe that Jesus was fully human and fully divine. He is alive today and vitally involves himself in human concerns. We affirm the goodness of Jesus' virgin birth, his miraculous activities, and his bodily resurrection. His triumph over the grave was the ultimate demonstration of his deity, which gives credibility to everything else he said and did while on earth.

An unfortunate consequence of the debate about Jesus' identity is that many people who believed in Jesus' divinity began to de-emphasize his teaching ministry. They were afraid that when people talked about Jesus' teaching, they were saying that this was all that mattered. Some branches of the church even claimed that large parts of his teaching, such as the Sermon on the Mount, do not apply to believers today. As a result, Jesus' importance as a teacher was largely passed over.

Jesus did not teach just to pass the time until the Crucifixion. His teachings are not an optional, dispensable part of his ministry. Rather, accepting him as a teacher is part of accepting him as Lord. Jesus' earliest followers were drawn to him primarily because his teaching made so much sense. He was the smartest man they had ever known. What he taught and modeled in his own life presented an accurate picture of reality. They had never seen anyone like him and had no idea that a life like his was even possible. Jesus was more than—but never less than—a trustworthy and credible teacher.

Because these early disciples trusted Jesus as their teacher, they were able to trust him as their Savior after his death and resurrection. If we want to fully experience Jesus' love, we must receive his teaching as one of his most important gifts. We must trust that he is right about everything and that when we disagree with him, either we are wrong or we do not yet completely understand what he is saying. Jesus must teach us how to live.

If you highly value the content of Jesus' teachings, you should find equal value in his teaching style and method. As parents, it will serve us well to pay attention to how Jesus dealt with his disciples. One of the best things he taught us was how to teach.

THE BRILLIANT HUMILITY OF JESUS

For some reason, Christians are quick to point out almost everything about Jesus except how smart he was. In *The Divine Conspiracy,* Dallas Willard writes, "The parables alone provide material that neither theologians nor philosophers can ever exhaust. This is a mark of Jesus' supreme genius. We have a curious tendency to overlook Jesus' sheer intellectual stature."[2]

Jesus was brilliant, but he never said things just to impress people or intentionally used his mind to make others feel inferior. He wasn't trying to make people aware of how great he was, but he wanted everyone who heard his words to put them into practice. He wanted each follower to bring glory to God by developing godly attitudes and character traits.

To accomplish these goals, Jesus used a variety of teaching strategies. He told stories, asked questions, and used common, everyday examples to reveal things about God. He allowed his disciples to be wrong without getting angry at them. He taught with gentleness and authority. He was the smartest man who ever lived, but he was also the most humble. His teaching ministry was not brilliant in spite of his humility but because of it.

Jesus' teaching is not intended only to enrich us intellectually. It does that, but head knowledge alone is insufficient. Learning from Jesus should make us more like him. Jesus rarely taught his followers things to do or not to do. Rather, he taught them new ways of seeing, thinking, and understanding. He knew that if people understood how things really worked, they might alter their behavior accordingly. Jesus is interested in our transformation, in our gradually becoming more like him in our thoughts and vision. This will lead to better behavior, but behavior is the effect, not the cause.

Dr. Jack Mezirow observed that people who go beyond merely learning information to actually transforming their worldviews go through these somewhat predictable stages:

There is an encounter with a "disorienting dilemma." This creates in them a sense of dissatisfaction with their present mindset or situation.

They examine themselves and their feelings of guilt, fear, or anger.

They question previously-held assumptions.

They explore alternative options.

They envision a new course of action.

They gather the necessary information and skill to move forward in this new course of action.

They "try on" new perspectives, roles, and behaviors to see how they fit.

They gain confidence and competence in these new roles and behaviors.

They reintegrate their newfound perspectives and ways of thinking into their lives.[3]

As this list shows, transformation is a process, not an event. Our becoming more like Jesus involves years of practice, of trial and error. Jesus' interactions with his disciples show how well he understood process-oriented transformation.

PARENTING FROM THE INSIDE OUT

Is there room in your parenting for humility? In other words, are you as a parent becoming more like Jesus? If we are going to effectively help our children connect with God, relate to others, and expand the borders of God's kingdom during their lives, we must take our cues from Jesus. If parents interact with their children without demonstrating the virtue of humility, something has gone terribly wrong.

Could this explain why so many parents are locked in a battle of wills with their children? Many parenting models are based on solid biblical material, but without the "mind of Christ"—the mind-set, attitude, and thoughtfulness of Jesus—passages from the Bible are often used to further authoritarian models of parenting that dishonor God and fail to produce the desired long-term results. Usually the verses that we are told should guide our parenting are used to support a power-based or indifferent stance toward children. "Good" children are those who obey—but often only passively and externally. This shortsighted definition of success makes parents feel good, but the long-term consequences are unbearable. These methods produce frightened, legalistic children rather than free and secure adults.

According to researcher George Barna, the average evangelical church in America loses 65 to 80 percent of its children by the time they reach their early twenties. Some of these children would have strayed regardless of their upbringing, but no one would find this an acceptable rate of attrition. Parents and church leaders like to think that all this is happening in spite of what they are doing, but there is a saying among systems analysts: "Your system is perfectly designed to produce the results you are getting." In other words, as difficult as it is to accept, the departure of young people from evangelical churches is happening, at least in part, *because* of what the churches are doing.

As children raised in an authoritarian environment grow older, they become less like Jesus and more like the legalistic, judgmental religious folks for whom Jesus reserved his harshest criticism. Others leave their faith altogether. Perhaps it would be better if the ones who stay were to go away too. Though nothing is more compelling, winsome, and valuable than well-lived Christianity, few things are as repulsive, destructive, or worthless as Christianity misunderstood and misapplied.

Gordon Smith, president of reSource Leadership International and former associate professor of spiritual theology at Regent College in Vancouver, British Columbia, shares a story about the need to love our children unconditionally in order to teach them about the love of God that transcends our behavior. He writes:

> Every year during the Christmas season as we do our mall shopping, we hear the piped-in Muzak that filters through the stores. We hear winter songs and Christmas carols, and invariably we hear "Santa Claus is Comin' to Town." This particularly insidious piece of music cuts at the heart of the gospel. It may sound like an innocent children's song, but consider the words:

> You better watch out, you better not cry,
> Better not pout, I'm telling you why:
> Santa Claus is comin' to town.

> He sees you when you're sleepin',
> He knows when you're awake,
> He knows if you've been bad or good,
> So be good for goodness' sake.

> What is the message? If we want to receive the benefits of Christmas, then we had better be good. If we are not good, then Santa Claus will know, and if he knows, there will be negative consequences.

> This is the very opposite of the Christmas message. The glory of Christmas is that Christ loved us while we were yet sinners. The whole point of Christmas is to celebrate God's love. "Santa Claus Is Comin' to Town" turns this on its head and thereby undermines the gospel.

> The perspective of this song resides deep in the heart of each person who has not accepted God's love. God loves us, and there is nothing we can do to make God love us more. All we can do is to accept, as a principle of faith, the fact that we are loved by God. We

believe this because Christ, the Son of God, died for us while we were still his enemies.

For many of us, our growing up experience was just the opposite of unconditional love. The fundamental assumption in our homes was that we would be loved if we behaved appropriately. How many children have assumed that if they wanted the love and blessing of their parents, they had to behave according to their parents' expectations?

As a parent, I know how difficult it is to love unconditionally without demanding that they change before they know my love and blessing. If either of my sons fails to fulfill some expectation of mine, it is easy to show my displeasure by standing aloof, withholding my blessing and making him feel as badly as I possibly can. Instead, if I express sorrow and perhaps even anger when something wrong is done, I must do so in a manner that never violates my first call to love my children. Knowing how difficult this is to do highlights the wonder of God's love for me. I must assure my sons of this love regardless of their behavior, for this is how God loves each of us.[4]

How different our homes would be if we stopped trying to make our children behave in certain ways and concentrated instead on showing them the unconditional love of God! Some people believe that this lifestyle is dangerous. They suppose that people who believe that they are loved regardless of their behavior will not be motivated to behave well. This unbiblical assumption does not correspond to how things work in the real world. Those who receive unconditional love are usually the most willing to behave in ways that meet with approval, precisely because they no longer need to earn it.

REDEFINING SUCCESS

What is our definition of successful parenting? In most cases, parents have the best of intentions for their children. Parents do not bring babies home from the hospital saying, "I can't wait to get this one home so I can mess up her life forever!" Parents want what is best for their kids, but they don't always have a clear understanding of what this means. Jesus does know, and that is precisely the point. Until we allow God to renew our minds, we will falsely define success for ourselves and our children, and this is very dangerous.

Jesus' definition of success includes moral behavior, but it doesn't stop there. Jesus is interested in our becoming the right kind of people, people for whom the right kind of behavior will come naturally. When we are thinking straight, we will no sooner defy the laws of God than defy the laws of gravity. According to Jesus, our definition of success isn't necessarily bad—it's just not good enough. He wants us to take the next step beyond behavior modification into character transformation. He expects this to influence the way we live and the way we parent our children.

Most of us have our own idea of what a good parenting job looks like. For some, it means quiet, well-behaved children who do their homework, make good grades, and generally stay out of trouble. For others, it means having outgoing and friendly children who manifest leadership qualities rather than merely following the crowd. For still others, it means having children who know the Bible, attend church, and pray regularly. For most Christian parents, it means having children who are developing their relationship with God. But why do we want children who are respectful, thoughtful, conscientious, and rightly related to God and other people? Why are those things near the center of our parenting targets?

Mostly it's because we want our kids to go to heaven. Parents don't find out they're expecting a child and say, "Great! Maybe this one will end up separated from God for all eternity." The mere thought of such a thing is horrific. Yet getting our kids into heaven, like the goal of external behavior modification, falls short of what God intends for his children. God's goal is not simply to get us into heaven; he also wants us to bring something of heaven into this dark world. We cannot have a lesser goal for our children.

What we already knew was a daunting challenge—raising moral, heaven-bound children in an immoral, hell-bent age—isn't just difficult, it's nearly impossible! Our task is to raise godly children who live in a godless environment but are not defined by it. Jesus' goal for his disciples was not that they would behave better, but that, while living in this world, they would allow their hearts and minds to be changed by the Spirit of God. Then they could take the earth-shatteringly good news of Jesus with them into the world, altering the course of human history.

Jesus' goal was lofty and seemingly unattainable given the raw materials his followers supplied, yet he pulled it off! There were times when it didn't look as if it would happen, but through Jesus' patience, diligence, and love, his band of brothers turned the world upside down. Within the span of a few generations, Christianity engendered the most powerful cultural revolution that the world has ever known.

We must reclaim the same objective for our children and our world. We must stop settling for better behavior and start raising children who are bold enough to believe that God has broken into our fallen world and redeemed it for his glory. In order to accomplish this, we need a solid strategy.

JESUS' STRATEGY

Because we have underestimated Jesus as a thinker, we may fail to realize that he didn't do things haphazardly. He knows the end from the beginning, and he had a plan when he called twelve men to be his disciples. He used his time with them as a launching process, and apparently he did rather well. After all, we are still talking about him, largely because of what his followers did and said after he was gone.

Jesus' strategy of exercising little control over his followers was particularly counterintuitive. It is important for us to grasp this as parents, because the more we try to control our children—especially as they enter adolescence—the more likely we are to push them away from us. Gary Thomas, founder and director of the Center for Evangelical Spirituality, shares an example of this from his own life:

My wife and son have been training our golden retriever puppy for the past several months. Recently, while on a walk, I saw my wife do something that surprised and impressed me. A short section of our trail ran next to a street, and our puppy wandered out toward some oncoming cars. In a panic, I rushed after Amber, which only encouraged her to go further in the wrong direction.

My wife kept her head and walked away from the danger. Suddenly Amber took an abrupt turn and went after Lisa, toward the safety of the trail. In the training process, Amber had learned that she should remain by Lisa's side. For a well-trained dog, its master is the most important piece of information. When Lisa turned, Amber knew she was supposed to turn, so when Lisa walked away from the danger, Amber instinctively followed.

Too many parents do what I did—chase their kids into the danger. Instead, we should take our cue from Lisa by walking away from the danger and inviting our kids to follow. Both Jesus and Paul did this, but it's very hard to do. Think for a moment about how concerned Jesus must have felt about leaving his church in the hands of a few cowering disciples. He knew that after his death, the disciples would gather behind locked doors, terrified and wondering what would become of them. He knew before he died that Peter, the "rock" on whom the young church would be built, would deny that he even knew Jesus—not once, but three times.

If he had been a fear-driven control freak, Jesus would never have gone to the cross because the disciples would never have been "ready enough." But Jesus let go. He trusted in the work of the Comforter, the Holy Spirit, to confirm the lessons he had taught— just as we have to trust the Holy Spirit to remind our children of the spiritual truths they have learned. Jesus returned to the Father, and though no one would claim that the church is perfect, it has survived and thrived for over two millennia.

The bachelor Jesus never physically fathered a child, but the process of parenting takes us to the same spiritual places that Jesus inhabited while he walked this earth.[5]

Jesus is the second member of the Trinity, the only begotten Son of God, the Alpha and Omega, and the one through whom and for whom all things were created and hold together. He demonstrated his power most completely in his ability to let his disciples go into the world without micromanaging their every decision and action! How was he able to do this?

According to Dr. Teresa Whitehurst in *How Would Jesus Raise a Child?* Jesus had three abilities that we should emulate in our parenting: He accepted the weaknesses of others, he refused to respond with impulsive anger, and he kept his eye on the final goal. When our children do things that drive us absolutely crazy, we can accept, as Jesus did, that our children sometimes behave in ways that we don't approve of. We can refuse to lose our temper when they do these things, and we can keep our minds on what is really important.

Accept the Weaknesses of Your Children

Few things are more innately powerful than acceptance. As most Christians know, we are born with a God-shaped hole in our hearts that can only be filled by God. In the opening pages of the Bible, we read of another hole—a human-shaped void that not even God will fill. God said that Adam was alone in the Garden before Eve was created. God described Adam, who enjoyed unbroken fellowship with God and who partnered with God on projects such as naming the animals and being a caretaker of the Garden, as being "alone." It's the first thing he ever called "not good."

All of us come into the world as terribly weak and desperately needy infants. None of us was self-sufficient when we were born. Children are the neediest, most self-absorbed, clingy, whiny, impatient people on the planet. Fortunately, some of us grow out of that, but paradoxically, the only way this can happen is for someone to accept us just the way we are without trying to change us.

People who claim to follow Jesus are often the least likely to accept the weaknesses of others. Jesus, the most righteous, holy, and perfectly behaved man to ever walk the earth, was so approachable and accepting that prostitutes, tax gougers, and shysters all ran to him. These same kinds of people now run away from his followers. Judgment and condemnation have become so deeply ingrained in us that we have a difficult time functioning without them. Nowhere does this have such a devastating impact as in our parenting. In *The Four Loves*, C. S. Lewis asks:

> Who has not been the embarrassed guest at family meals where the father or mother treated their grown-up offspring with an incivility which, offered to any other young people, would simply have terminated the acquaintance? Dogmatic assertions on matters which the children understand and their elders don't, ruthless interruptions, flat contradictions, ridicule of things the young take seriously, . . . insulting references to their friends, all provide an easy answer to the question, "Why are they always out? Why do they like every house better than their home?" Who does not prefer civility to barbarism?[6]

Accepting our children with all of their weaknesses is not the same as being tolerant or approving of their foolish behavior. Our children need more than that. Jesus did not simply put up with his disciples through gritted teeth or treat them as if he were doing them a favor. From all appearances, Jesus actually seemed to like them, even when they messed up.

Jesus accepted those who came to him—women, men, Jews, Gentiles, sinners—with a completely undeserved acceptance. And yet his acceptance was demanding. There were no prerequisites to his acceptance, but his acceptance accomplished what condemnation and judgment never could. His acceptance inspired the kind of change from within that we long to see in ourselves and our children. What would happen in our homes if we began to practice this level of acceptance with our children? In *Love beyond Reason*, John Ortberg shares a story about one of his daughters:

We used to have a bedtime ritual when my children were small. "I don't love you this much," I'd say, holding my hands a few inches apart, "and I don't love you this much" (hands a foot apart now), "or this much, or this much" (the gap growing wider until it was as far as my arms could go). "I love you this much."

Occasionally, they would test it. We were washing the car when one of my children got into the trunk, put all its contents on the ground, and sprayed them thoroughly; books, blankets, my tennis racquet, and a new dress were all hosed and sudsed up beyond recognition. My daughter, who was about four at the time, could see from my face that she had sinned, and that the wages of sin is death. She looked up with big brown eyes and threw her arms out to the side as far as she could: "I love you this much."

How could I punish that? "All right, honey. Let's just put this stuff in the garage."[7]

It's not difficult to imagine the bond strengthening between father and daughter in that moment. This little girl will grow up with a good understanding of who God is and how he has accepted her. As a young woman, she will be far more likely to extend that same level of acceptance to others—and perhaps nudge them closer to their heavenly Father.

Refuse to Respond with Impulsive Anger

Suppose that in the above story John Ortberg had blasted his daughter, said that she was a bad girl, and sent her to her room without any supper. What message would that communicate to a four-year-old? It would indicate that Daddy is out of control.

Anger is sometimes appropriate. Usually, however, our anger is fueled by our own insecurities and fears. That's why the Bible tells us, "Everyone should be quick to listen, slow to speak and slow to become angry, for man's anger does not bring about the righteous life that God desires" (James 1:19-20). Until you can say that your anger is godly, it is probably best to keep it to yourself.

Anger is a problem for most parents from time to time. Adults who are otherwise calm and even-tempered can be reduced to raving maniacs in a matter of minutes by childish behavior. Parental anger fails to bring about the righteous life that God desires; it usually also fails to bring about a favorable change in our children's behavior. Children sometimes become immune to our angry outbursts or learn how to turn their anger on us—fighting fire with fire. We're successfully training them to have anger-management issues, just like the ones Mom and Dad have.

Studies show that angry outbursts are on the rise. Apparently rage is all the rage among young people, as they are shown that the one with the shortest fuse or the biggest explosion wins at home. But if it takes blowing up to get your children to do what you want, you're always going to have to blow up to get your children to do what you want. They won't know that you're serious until the explosion. By responding with impulsive anger, you enslave yourself to that pattern and keep setting yourself up to repeat it.

Our impulsive anger frightens our children and robs them of the security that comes from knowing that at least one of us has a handle on a given situation. More than anything else, our children want us to be grown-ups, people who practice self-control. As marriage and family therapist Hal Runkel says, "If you're not under control, then you cannot be in charge."[8] Screaming until we're blue in the face makes us look foolish. Parents have to take responsibility for their own emotional outbursts. No one can "make" anyone angry, and if your buttons are being pushed by a toddler, it's time for a time-out—for you, not the toddler.

Angry outbursts are not good for us. They don't work. They scare our children and make us look foolish. Yet for some strange reason, we keep trying to intimidate our children into behaving properly. Can you imagine what it would be like if God did that? What if every time we disobeyed or doubted, God blew up, puffed out his chest, and told us that if we didn't straighten up and fly right, there'd be nothing left but a grease spot when he got through with us?

The biggest problem with impulsive anger is that it's ungodly. God is often angry, but he's never impulsive. He acts thoughtfully and intentionally, usually curbing his anger and tempering it with mercy. Anyone who talks about God's wrath outside of the context of God's love isn't reading the Bible correctly. Anyone who parents out of anger instead of love isn't parenting the way Jesus would.

Keep Your Eye on the Final Goal

"Do you not know that in a race all the runners run, but only one gets the prize? Run in such a way as to get the prize" (1 Corinthians 9:24). Paul's words to the church in Corinth came from his understanding of how Jesus lived. When Jesus taught, he kept his goal firmly in mind. He knew that his objective was much more important than just changing the disciples' behavior. He changed who they were and how they thought, knowing full well that their behavior would eventually correct itself. Rather than allow himself to be distracted by momentary lapses, Jesus applauded positive movement toward the greater goal.

How many stories have you heard about successful people who never saw a complicated objective as unattainable? People whom we call great heroes had this strength of character. Christopher Columbus was determined to find the New World. Abraham Lincoln lost practically everything he tried to achieve, except the presidency. Lance Armstrong battled cancer and won the Tour de France—seven times. These people are our heroes because they had their eyes on the end purpose, not on the impediments that surrounded them.

The great heroes that we should tell our children about have helped to fill the God-shaped hole and the people-shaped hole in someone else's heart. Atlanta's Ashley Smith, a single mom who didn't always make the right choices, was held hostage in her own home. Even as her captor held a gun to her head, she pointed him toward Jesus, compelling him to confront the gaping hole inside him that needed to be filled. Now *that's* keeping your eyes on the real goal!

Instead of screaming in fear, Smith challenged this man to think about his identity and his thought process. Rather than allow herself to be distracted by her captor's judgment, she applauded anything positive she saw in him. You may know the rest of the story: *He let her go and turned himself in.* Smith wasn't sure if that would happen, but God enabled her to keep her wits about her until her captor could be persuaded. Her daughter will grow up knowing that her mother risked her life for her child and for her captor's soul. That is good parenting!

Another mom tells a triumphant story about the love for Jesus that was instilled in her daughter as a child. In the years since the Columbine High School massacre of April 1999, many have heard the story of Misty Bernall's daughter, Cassie, who was questioned about her belief in Jesus and was then shot and killed in the school's library. Misty's book, *She Said Yes,* honestly recounts the turmoil in Cassie's life—the bad choices, the questionable friends, and the profound depression against which her daughter struggled. Eventually Cassie broke free of those things, and at the one climactic moment when nothing else mattered but life, she drew upon Christ's character. Misty writes, "The real issue raised by Cassie's death is not what she said to her killers, but what it was that enabled her to face them as she did. I'm not saying she consciously prepared herself for a terrible end. She didn't have a death wish, I'm sure, and it would be obscene to suggest otherwise. Yet when tragedy struck her out of the blue, she remained calm and courageous. She was ready to go."[9]

According to her mother, Cassie would have hated to be singled out and held up as a shining example of martyrdom. But we live in a world that needs to hear stories like Cassie's. We know she wasn't a perfect little saint, yet she offered her life in the name of the Perfect One. And as much as we grieve her death, we can be proud of Cassie for her example.

> I'm profoundly proud of her for refusing to cave in, and for saying yes to her killers, and I always will be. She had principles and morals, and she was not ashamed of them, even though it must have taken all the courage she could muster to hold fast. When I first heard what she had done, I looked at [my husband] Brad, and

I wondered, "Would I have done that?" I might have begged for my life. Cassie didn't. She may have been seventeen, but she's a far stronger woman than I'll ever be.[10]

We believe that Misty's words are heartfelt, but regarding her perception that her own faith was weaker than her daughter's, we think she sells herself short. After all, Cassie grew up in a loving Christian home, where she watched her mother and father live out their faith. According to her peers and friends of the family, Cassie learned her faith from her parents. A parent's most tragic thought is of the loss of a child, yet Misty Bernall challenges us to teach our children to "say yes." They will learn it best by seeing that "yes" in our daily example, as we keep our eyes on the final goal.

Many authorities on childhood offer valuable counsel on handling your child's development, but none can ensure your child's reaction to your labors. Maybe one of our goals as parents should be to ignore how smart we are. When a child needs to be guided in the right direction, we can defer our brilliant response to the Suffering Servant, who truly knows the answer. This servant will not chase us into the street, yelling, "Come back here! How many times do I have to tell you to watch out for traffic?" No, he simply expects us to hear his voice and trust him enough to follow its sound back to safety. He does not sing, "You'd better watch out," but watches us fumble around like fools, laughs kindly at our badly informed antics, and throws his arms open wide, because he loves us—*that much.*

That is some unconditional love!

Don't our children deserve as much from us?

part 2
What We Believe

In this section, we discuss a Christian worldview—how to develop it, live it, and pass it on. The most important thing is to know what you believe. We'll talk about what it means to truly believe in God, why that is a good choice, and what the logical conclusions of that decision mean for your life and the lives of your children. If God is who he says he is, it follows that he defines reality and the meaning of life. If we acknowledge this, we can come to peace with an issue that most of the world will struggle to understand or will avoid altogether.

Think about your personal possessions. Make a mental catalog of all your belongings—your home, vehicles, jewelry, furniture, cameras, computers, checking account, savings account, stocks, bonds—the whole lot. If you were to have a garage sale today, how much would you get for all of it?

All of the stuff that clogs up your attic and clutters up your closets is actually worth something. Some of it might be worth quite a bit, and perhaps you are better off for having it. You live differently according to whether you do or do not own a car. Your existence is to some extent defined by whether you have shoes, a house, a computer, or other things you might consider the bare necessities of modern life. The things that you have change the way that you live.

Now turn to your personal ideas—your concepts and beliefs, your views about what is genuine and valuable in this world. Think for a moment about your notion of God, yourself, and others, and how they all fit together. Consider the values and morals by which you live. How much are they worth? Is there any way to assess their significance? Is your life different because of your beliefs?

Of course it is. Our possessions, ideas, and beliefs all influence the way that we live. This has always been the case and probably doesn't surprise you. Centuries ago, Europeans believed that they were naturally superior to Africans, and based on this belief they perpetuated and rationalized the slave trade. It made slavery sound like a positive good rather than a necessary evil—after all, it allowed inferior people a place in society.[1] The Holocaust also occurred as the result of certain ideas, not just the use of force. Nazi soldiers, for the most part, weren't forced to commit atrocities against women and children. They simply had to be convinced that cruelty was sometimes necessary in order to realize the greater good of a revived and prosperous Germany.

Ideas have consequences.

WHAT IS A *WELTANSCHAUUNG?*

As Christians, we hold certain beliefs to be true. For example, we believe that abortion is morally wrong because humans, having been created in the image of God, are inherently valuable. For the same reason, we ought to closely watch the current debate regarding euthanasia. Perhaps we should also examine our views on capital punishment and "just war" theories, just to make sure that we are being consistent. We believe that murder is wrong because we believe in the sanctity of human life. Lying is wrong because we believe that God is a truthful being and truthful behavior on our part best reflects his character. Our reasons for allowing or disallowing certain actions are based upon our central belief systems. We decide whether or not these actions can be reconciled with a biblically informed worldview.

But what exactly is a worldview? Not long ago, this word was something of a mystery, but now it's hard to browse a bookshelf without seeing it. We typed the word *worldview* into amazon.com and found 405 items! How did this word come to its place of prominence in our contemporary vocabulary? What exactly does it mean? If a worldview is so important, how can we make sure that we have the correct one? What can we do as parents to ensure that our children develop theirs appropriately?

The Germans were the first to name this quest for a unified, systematic way of looking at the universe, and notable among them was the philosopher Immanuel Kant. He called it *Weltanschauung*—literally, "look onto the world." Whereas our English translation of the word tends to be associated with physical nature, this German technical term represents the widest view the mind can take in order to grasp the world as a whole from the standpoint of some philosophy.[2]

The meaning of the term *worldview* seems self-evident: It is an intellectual perspective on the world or the universe. But ask a dozen philosophers and theologians to define it, and you are likely to get a dozen different answers. For example, in "The Question of a *Weltanschauung*" from his *New Introductory Lectures on Psycho-Analysis,* Sigmund Freud described a worldview as "an intellectual construction which solves all the problems of our existence uniformly on the basis of one overriding hypothesis, which, accordingly, leaves no question unanswered and in which everything that interests us finds its fixed place."[3] Though it would be nice if we could find some intellectual construct that would solve all of our existential problems, perhaps we shouldn't hold our breath.

In *Types and Problems of Philosophy,* Hunter Mead suggests that a worldview is "a somewhat poetic term to indicate either an articulated system of philosophy or a more or less unconscious attitude toward life and the world."[4] In an article on philosopher Wilhelm Dilthey in *The Encyclopedia of Philosophy,* H. P. Rickman says that a worldview is a philosophy "in which a picture of reality is combined with a sense of its meaning and value and with principles of action."[5]

Christian thinkers have also weighed in on the subject. Notably, James W. Sire has written that a worldview is simply a "set of presuppositions (assumptions which may be true, partially true, or entirely false) which we hold (consciously or subconsciously, consistently or inconsistently) about the basic makeup of the world."[6]

Lest we think this is a new concept, Arthur F. Holmes reminds us that "the quest for a unifying worldview that will help us to see life whole and find meaning in each part is as old as humankind. . . . The human need for a worldview . . . is fourfold: the need to unify thought and life; the need to define the good life and find hope and meaning in life; the need to guide thought; the need to guide action."[7]

Got it? Okay, make sure that you have the right worldview and skip ahead to the next chapter. Isn't that how Christian books sometimes go? They assume that you know what a worldview is, which ones are biblical, and how to change or adapt yours to bring it more in line with what the Bible has to say about God, you, and the world in which you live. We dare not make these dangerous assumptions. The stakes are too high to merely state the obvious (especially if the obvious is quite obscure) and move on. Instead, we'd like to cut through all the academic language and give you a practical definition of a worldview.

PRACTICALLY SPEAKING

Think of your worldview as a really comfortable pair of eyeglasses. If your glasses are comfortable enough, you can actually forget that you're wearing them. You can go through life without constantly thinking, "These glasses are helping me understand the world around me, read street signs, watch television, and read this book." Rather, you simply take for granted that you can see.

Some glasses are also fashion accessories. Anyone who has ever purchased a pair of glasses knows that the real cost is not in the eye exam or the lenses, but in the frames. If you go to your local mall to get a pair of glasses, the clerks will ask you all kinds of questions: What looks best with the shape of your face? What colors work well with your skin tones? Which materials do you prefer—metals, plastics, or a combination? What type of look are you after—bold, conservative, artsy, all business?

Not one of these questions addresses the real issue of being able to see things accurately. Glasses are supposed to be more than just comfortable and stylish. It's great when they are, but that's not their purpose. Ugly, uncomfortable glasses of the correct prescription are superior to comfortable and attractive glasses that don't help you see things as they really are.

Whether you know it or not, you go through life seeing things through a certain set of lenses. They may be accurate or inaccurate. They may be politically correct or old-fashioned. They may be so comfortable that you forget you're wearing them, but they're there nonetheless. You see the world the way you do and interpret events and statements in particular ways because of them. You act the way you act, vote the way you vote, and to a large extent feel the way you feel because of the way that you view the world. Dr. Armand Nicholi Jr. writes the following:

> Our worldview informs our personal, social, and political lives. It influences how we perceive ourselves, how we relate to others, how we adjust to adversity, and what we understand to be our purpose. Our worldview helps determine our values, our ethics, and our capacity for happiness. It helps us understand where we come from, our heritage; who we are, our identity; why we exist on this planet, our purpose; what drives us, our motivation; and where we are going, our destiny. . . . Our worldview tells more about us perhaps than any other aspect of our personal history.[8]

Obviously, a worldview is not just theoretically important; there are intensely practical reasons for us to consider the issue, especially as parents. With an improperly formed worldview, children will never come to grips with who they are, where they came from, where they're going, what's wrong with the world, or what God's solutions are to the problems of our lives. What we really believe about these deepest issues is made clear by what we do. As Dallas Willard rightly noted, "The reason why clergy and others have to invest so much effort into getting people to *do* things is that they are working against the actual beliefs of the people they are trying to lead."[9]

It's not just clergy, is it? It's parents too. Parents often struggle with getting their children to behave in certain ways because they tend to overlook and underestimate the power of what their children actually believe. We must not ignore the sources of our children's core beliefs or the role we play in shaping them, for no one has as much opportunity to influence the heart of a child—for good or bad—as a parent. As we consider a Christian worldview, we must realize that if we want our children to possess such a framework for interpreting their universe, we must first hold this worldview ourselves. It has to be in us before we can instill it in our kids. Moses said, "These commandments . . . are to be upon your hearts" *before* he said, "Impress them on your children" (Deuteronomy 6:6-7).

FIGURING OUT WHAT YOU REALLY BELIEVE

You do not choose most of your beliefs. That may sound strange, but it's true. If you could choose your beliefs, you could change them at will. Try, for example, believing that the United States did not win independence from Great Britain. You could *say* that the United States is still under British rule. You could even *act* as if that were the case. But would you really believe it—deep down in that place where you believe what you believe? Probably not.

This doesn't mean that you have an insufficient imagination. It just tells us something about the nature of beliefs. In some ways, our beliefs choose us. But this is not to say that we are powerless when it comes to our beliefs. There are things we can do—activities around which we can orient our lives—so that over time our beliefs can be shaped by these actions and the resulting experiences. But we cannot arbitrarily choose to believe certain things.

So how do we figure out what we really believe? According to Michael Wittmer, associate professor of systematic theology at Grand Rapids Theological Seminary, it helps to think of your worldview as a series of concentric circles.[10] Every belief that you hold is attached—at least indirectly—to every other belief you hold, but some beliefs are deeper and more central than others. Those most central beliefs form the core of your worldview; those that are further out are easier to abandon.

Here's an example: You may believe that it is sunny outside even though you cannot see outside right now. If someone were to ask you why you believe that it's sunny, you might say, "The weather report this morning said it was sunny, and I believe the weather report to be trustworthy."

Suppose that person replied, "But haven't you been watching the news? The weather report has changed, and they are now saying that it's raining outside." Now you must change your belief, but which one changes first? You might discard your belief that it is sunny outside but maintain your belief that the weather report is trustworthy.

If, however, you are standing in the rain while listening to the weather report tell you that it's sunny outside, you are likely to change your belief that the weather report is trustworthy. Why would you make that change? Simply put, you believe that your senses are more trustworthy than the weather report.

If you were to ask yourself why you believe that your senses are more trustworthy than the weather report, how would you respond? This is getting tricky now, isn't it? Perhaps you believe that your senses are trustworthy because you are created in God's image and he has created your senses to function properly. But why do you believe that?

If you ask yourself why you believe what you believe, and another belief surfaces, ask yourself why you believe that one. Eventually you'll hit a stopping point—a point at which you simply throw up your hands and say, "I believe it because I just do." Stop there. That's your ultimate presupposition. That's the very center of your worldview. And here's the reason why this is important: You always reason *from* this center, not *toward* it. In other words, our ultimate presuppositions determine the way that we interpret the world around us. Our experiences do not shape our worldview; it's the other way around.

It's not unusual to see several people go through the exact same experience and yet have different perspectives on what happened. Why? One reason is that they have different worldviews, different ultimate presuppositions. Three people may survive an automobile crash. One believes that God was getting back at him for not tithing. One believes that it was just bad luck, a case of being in the wrong place at the wrong time. The third believes that God was gracious to her in preventing the wreck from being any worse than it was.

Who's correct? More to the point, how would you go about convincing one or more of these people that they were incorrect?[11] The way people react to their circumstances is a direct result of their core beliefs, and circumstances actually reinforce these beliefs.[12] The man in the accident who thinks that God is out to get him feels guilty for not tithing, and he believes that God is vengeful and punishes us here on earth. Getting in a wreck confirms this idea for him. Why would this happen if God were not out to get him?

Clearly, what matters most is not what happens to us, but how we interpret what happens to us. Having a proper worldview—a Christian worldview—enables us to endure suffering with joy, disappointment with peace, and grief with hope. Having a faulty worldview, with values and behaviors that are theologically warped because they do not have God at their center, does not cause bad things to happen to us, but it does breed negative emotions such as guilt, cynicism, and despair. The secret to a satisfying life is not to avoid unpleasant experiences (you can't!) but to have a worldview that allows you to interpret them correctly.

GETTING DOWN TO BRASS TACKS

Let's address the basic questions that a worldview must answer. Many scholars and writers have compiled lists of such questions, but we are not concerned simply with how we should live but how we should live *as parents*. We will confine our discussion to how parents can help their children see life through the lens of a Christian worldview. These questions are not exhaustive. If you're interested in learning more about the ramifications of your worldview, you will find several good resources listed at the end of the book.

The basic questions a worldview must answer include the following:

1. Who am I?
2. Where am I?
3. How did I get here?
4. Why am I here?
5. What's wrong with me and my world?
6. Is there a solution to this problem?

Entire books have been written to answer these questions. We will not be able to treat each question fully, but it is vitally important for us as parents to have a working knowledge of these issues if we are to help our children navigate the difficult waters in the inquisitive stage of faith development.

Who Am I?

There are two basic answers to this question. Human beings are either the accidental product of impersonal, evolutionary processes, or they are intentionally created beings. Put simply, we either came about as a result of chance plus time, or we were purposefully created by someone or something. We'll talk about that "purposeful creator" later. For now, we must face the question of our identity. The best science, the best philosophy, and the best theology all tell us that we are not accidental by-products of a mindless universe.

The Bible tells us that humans were originally created by God, in his image, to enjoy a relationship with him. The creation account in Genesis tells us that humans are the pinnacle of God's creation. There is a clear difference, biblically speaking, between humans and other animals or plants. We are not God, but as beings created in his image, we are given a level of authority over our planet that puts us in a position of great honor.[13]

Being human is amazing. Most of us have astounding abilities of vision, hearing, touch, taste, and smell. We can think about our world and formulate judgments about it. We can know true from false, good from bad, and beautiful from ugly. We feel profound emotions such as love, joy, hate, discouragement, hope, and gratitude. We reason and plan our lives in such a way that things are accomplished.

One of the best things about having a dog is realizing that you're not one. Dogs seem kind, forgiving, humble, and warm. But they're dogs! A dog doesn't understand or reason as we do. Dogs do not seem to care where they came from. They do not reflect on their unique personal identity or wonder what it means to be a dog in God's scheme of things.

They don't think about why they're here, and they don't know where they are going.

Dogs can invite a lot of affection, but they are not humans created in the image of God. Dogs are wonderful, but humans are much more amazing. Some dog lovers find these creatures captivating, but what about the humans who constantly surround us? Human beings have indescribable mysteries awaiting them at every turn. Each has an eternal destiny of unspeakable joy or overwhelming horror.

Realizing this can either press you down with fear and trembling or buoy you up with peace and hope. Whether it does the one or the other depends in large measure on how you answer this question: Who am I? No animal ever lost one night's sleep contemplating this. Only humans require a true and satisfying answer to this question.

We are intentionally created beings, made in God's image for his glory, designed to be stewards over the rest of God's creation, and intended to enjoy deep friendship with God and with other humans. No other worldview—religious, cultural, or philosophical—provides us with such a deep and fulfilling understanding of what it means to be human. No other worldview offers us the humility of being part of the created order and the honor of being created in the image of the Creator. Get this wrong, and it's like getting the top button on your shirt wrong: Nothing else will line up properly.

Where Am I?

This question also has two basic answers. Either we are clinging to an accidental ball of dust orbiting around a star at a rate of 67,000 miles per hour, or we are standing firmly and confidently on a planet that was specifically designed to be inhabited by people.

The Bible says that we live in a world created by the One in whose image we were created. God, who has pretty high standards, looked at the world he had created and pronounced, "It is good." He did not say, "That's good enough." Any attempts—Christian or otherwise—to deny the goodness and beauty of this earth are to be rejected as Gnostic heresy.[14]

God is good, and he created a good universe—not a neutral or inherently evil one.

The planet Earth is an amazing place, filled with sights, sounds, and mysteries that keep the sharpest minds constantly in awe. For instance, the energy in one hurricane is equal to about five hundred thousand atomic bombs. The Marianas Trench in the Pacific Ocean is so deep that Mount Everest could be submerged in it with its summit still more than a mile below the surface. The oceans contain more than six hundred million cubic miles of water. In the middle of the Atlantic Ocean, two tectonic plates—the African and the North American—are moving apart at about the same speed that your fingernails grow. The center of the earth's core is thought to be nearly the same temperature as the surface of the sun. Impressed with this place yet?

What about the diversity of flowers and trees that our planet sustains? The green of springtime just after a rain is like nothing we could conjure up on our own. The smell of fresh-cut grass and the spray of mist from a waterfall are but two examples of God's wonderful creativity. God's creation is utterly good, and it is meant to be enjoyed, cultivated, and wisely tended.[15] God commissioned humans to be stewards of his creation, and no one should enjoy and protect nature more than Christians.

How Did I Get Here?

Either we got here on purpose, or it was all a big accident. Theists believe that humans were intentionally placed on this earth by an intelligent Designer. As the first Vatican Council (1870) put it, God created everything "by his goodness and omnipotent excellence, not to augment or add to his beatitude, but to manifest his perfection by the good things which he imparts to creatures, by entirely free design."[16] Or as Protestant Louis Berkhof wrote, "Creation in the strict sense of the word may be defined as that free act of God whereby He, according to His sovereign will and for His own glory, in the beginning brought forth the whole visible and invisible universe."[17]

Darwinists believe that "man is the result of a purposeless and natural process that did not have him in mind. He was not planned."[18]

These proposed answers are mutually exclusive. If one is true, the other must be false. Everything in our belief system depends on how we answer this question. Nearly a century ago, Catholic theologian Joseph Pohle said, "Unless we know God as the Creator of all things, we do not know the true God."[19] The whole Christian faith rests upon this foundation, which is why so much research and energy are poured into answering this question from a Christian perspective. In the words of American theologian Langdon Gilkey, "The idea that God is the Creator of all things is the indispensable foundation on which the other beliefs of the Christian faith are based. It affirms what the Christian believes about the status of God in the whole realm of reality: He is the Creator of everything else. On this affirmation logically depends all that Christians say about their God, about the world they live in, and about their own history, destiny, and hope."[20]

If we are just happy accidents, then we are not accountable. There is no reason why we should think of suffering as inferior to flourishing, no rational expectation of justice, no meaning or purpose in our living, and no transcendent hope in our dying. We are free to create our own definitions of true and false, good and bad, beautiful and ugly, and we have no one to blame but ourselves for the mess we're in. Such a view of life is not only miserable, but it is increasingly difficult to maintain in light of the arguments that solid Christian scholars are making.[21]

Why Am I Here?

If we are on this earth as the result of chance plus time, then there is no overarching reason for our existence. We are merely the products of what Richard Dawkins calls "the blind watchmaker"—a mysterious and unknowable force that seems to create order without purpose.[22]

If, however, we are created beings purposefully placed in our present world, then we are wise to invest time and energy in discovering why.

There is some debate over this answer, even among Christians. One approach is to say that God created us for our sake; another is to say that God created us for his own sake. We believe that both sides are correct. God created us out of his *goodness* for the sake of his *glory*.

God created the world to express his goodness and to share his love with creatures made in his own image.[23] The Bible teaches that God created nature for humanity's good, so part of our reason for being here, according to the Christian tradition, is to enjoy and wisely manage the splendor and beauty of creation.[24]

The ultimate goodness that God bestows upon us is a personal relationship with him. Because we are created in God's image, we are personal beings who can know and relate to God in an "I/Thou" relationship. The blessings of nature are to be enjoyed specifically as gifts of God's love. Regardless of the presence or absence of material blessings in this world, we can maintain a sense of transcendent joy as long as we remain connected to God, because in his presence is "fullness of joy" (Psalm 16:11, NKJV).[25]

This ultimate goodness of being connected to God in a personally satisfying relationship overflows into a renewed ability to relate properly to those around us. Only as we are connected to God can we explore the depths of human intimacy. The level of relational difficulties and the ease with which relationships are dissolved in our world reveals a serious disconnection, not just among people but between people and God. The truth is that we are all disconnected from God. We have a hard time maintaining connectedness with each other, and we're doing a poor job of relating to nature as well. The Christian worldview is the only system of belief that offers a satisfactory explanation for all of these problems.

Though God created the world to bless the hearts of rational creatures with the goodness of his love, he also created it to manifest his glory in creation and to be glorified by it. This is clearly seen throughout the Bible.[26] God created simply for the joy and satisfaction that he receives from the works of his own hands. God's highest purpose—to be glorified—is fulfilled in the highest possible way through the creation of persons in his own image. These personal beings can acknowledge God's glory as manifested in his works and can praise and adore him for this. The Westminster Catechism begins with the question, "What is the chief end of man?" The answer it gives is, "To glorify God, and to enjoy Him forever."[27]

What's Wrong with Me and My World?

If we are merely overgrown germs that accidentally landed on a purposeless planet, then nothing is wrong with individuals or the world in which we live. In fact, nothing is wrong with anything. Without a transcendent standard of rightness, we are duplicitous in speaking of things as being wrong. For example, Darwinist Richard Dawkins writes, "In a universe of blind physical forces and genetic replication, some people are going to get hurt, other people are going to get lucky, and you won't find any rhyme or reason in it, nor any justice. The universe we observe has precisely the properties we should expect if there is, at bottom, no design, no purpose, no evil and no good, nothing but blind, pitiless indifference."[28] And yet there is something deep within even the most hardened skeptics that cries out, *Things are not the way they're supposed to be.*

Philosopher and theologian Cornelius Plantinga Jr. has written a brilliant treatment of this theme. In his book *Not the Way It's Supposed to Be,* he reminds us that "central in the classic Christian understanding of the world is a concept of the way things are supposed to be."[29] We are created in God's image, invested with divine glory, and ordained to rule as stewards over creation. We are supposed to live in intimate relationship with one another and with God, individually and corporately making responsible choices that honor and glorify him. But, as Plantinga writes,

> Of course, things are not that way at all. Human wrongdoing, or the threat of it, mars every adult's workday, every child's school day, every vacationer's holiday. A moment's reflection yields a whole catalogue of wrongdoing, some of it so familiar we scarcely think of it any longer as wrong: a criminal in a forties film noir hangs up a pay telephone receiver and then, before exiting the

booth, rips from the telephone book a page he had consulted and pockets it. At school, a third grader in a class of twenty-five distributes fifteen party invitations in a manner calculated to let the omitted classmates clearly see their exclusion. Her teacher notes but never ponders the social dynamics of this distribution scheme. Two old flames meet again for the first time since graduation and begin to muse with nostalgia and boozy self-pity over what might have been. Though each feels happily married to someone else, somehow the evening climaxes for the two grads in a room at the Marriott.[30]

It didn't take much imagination for Plantinga to write this. Any one of us could sit down and "in a moment's reflection" bring to mind a laundry list of problems—trivial wrongs, tragic events, and corruption on a grand scale—that scar our landscape and prevent us from experiencing God's purpose in creation. G. K. Chesterton once called original sin the only Christian doctrine that could be empirically verified by thousands of years of human history. He was correct, and most of our sins are far from original. Humans seem content to endlessly repeat the same sinful patterns.

The world is disordered. We do not experience the peace and prosperity God originally intended—our relationships quickly deteriorate, and our planet groans under the strain of our collectively irresponsible choices. We have strayed from our original design. The word that describes this may seem old-fashioned and archaic, but it is true: The problem is *sin*.

We have missed the target, strayed from the path, and wandered from the fold. We have been weighed in the balance and come up short. We are hard-hearted, stiff-necked, blind, deaf, and dumb. We have crossed the line and failed to measure up. We don't merely engage in sinful behavior—though we do that, oftentimes, with reckless abandon. We sin because we are sinners.

As much as we want to avoid unpleasantness, life has a way of bringing us back to this reality of sin and our need to confront it. In *Explaining Hitler,* Ron Rosenbaum looks at various popular scholarly theories of the last fifty years that attempt to explain the atrocities committed by Adolph Hitler. Ultimately no explanation can provide a satisfactory rationale for this "smiling," bloodthirsty dictator who by all accounts fully understood the depth of his own malice. Hitler didn't have to kill Jews, Poles, or homosexuals. He was not under compulsion from any outside force. He carried out the Holocaust because on some level he wanted to. This evil man operated from a worldview that deeply affected his values and behaviors. His Nazi supporters were apparently wearing similar "comfortable" glasses that convinced them cruelty was acceptable.

In truth, we are all evil men and women. Though it is convenient for us to point the finger at some external source of misery and say, "Ah, there's the problem: sin!" it is more effective to confront the person staring back at us in the mirror. The problem is not something strange out there, but something familiar within. *The London Times* once asked people to respond to the question, "What is wrong with the world?" G. K. Chesterton wrote this reply:

> Dear Sirs,
> I am.
> Sincerely yours,
> G. K. Chesterton

What is wrong with us is that each of us is a sinner. What is wrong with our world is that each of us is a sinner. Thankfully, God has not washed his hands of us. He already has a plan in force to set our upsidedown world right side up again.

Is There a Solution to This Problem?

Depending on which path we took at the first crossroads ("Who am I?"), we might still say, "What problem?" But it seems that most people are willing to admit—however grudgingly—that the world is in a poor state. Some people believe that humans are nothing more than accidents of nature, residing on this third rock from the sun for no known reason, but even they recognize that conditions are not ideal. Their solutions to our man-made problems are equally man-made and equally problematic.

As social critic Henry Fairlie observed, the fields of psychology and sociology merely contend that "our . . . faults and those of our societies are the result of some kind of mechanical failure, which has only to be diagnosed and understood for us to set it right."[31] Because the world has no transcendent source of truth, the primitive idea that sin is the cause of our social ills seems out of place. We have become a people who largely reject the idea that anyone should determine right and wrong objectively—even if that "anyone" is God.

We can take heart in the fact that the Christian worldview offers a solution to our crisis. God, who created all things and stepped back to proclaim them "very good," will not allow us to deface his property for long. As surely as the Creation was followed by the Fall, God prepared and enacted redemption. Cornelius Plantinga writes, "To speak of sin by itself, to speak of it apart from the realities of creation and grace, is to forget the resolve of God. God wants shalom and will pay any price to get it back. Human sin is stubborn, but not as stubborn as the grace of God and not half so persistent, not half so ready to suffer to win its way."[32]

God is at work, redeeming sinners who have seemingly ruined their lives beyond repair. He refuses to allow sin to have the last word, so he works tirelessly in all kinds of ways to bring about his Kingdom. We cannot solve our own problems because our solutions are humanly devised and empowered. God's solution will triumph because it depends on his ability—not ours. Do you *believe* that?

If someone asked you if you "believed in" George W. Bush, you might think that person was joking. *Of course* you believe in George W. Bush! He's the president, for goodness sake. You've see him on television, and you know he is in Washington, D.C., trying to lead the country. You believe what you see. If that same person asked if you "knew" George W. Bush, you might say, "No. I've never met him." You haven't spent time with him, you don't jog together, and you've never asked his wife to pass you the salt from across the dinner table. There is a difference between believing that someone exists and actually *knowing* that person. *Do you merely believe in God or do you actually know God?* Is he only a part of the values and behaviors of your life, or is he at the *center* of your worldview?

ARE WE STILL TALKING ABOUT PARENTING?

We've taken a difficult hike into rarified philosophical air in this chapter. You may be thinking, *This sure is interesting, but how does it help me with my kids?* Let's connect the dots before we move on to the next chapter.

Our worldview is the lens through which we see ourselves and our place in this world. The Bible says that we see things through a fog right now (1 Corinthians 13:12). Often when we try to make sense of human suffering and tragic events, the best we can do is guess. We can make out shapes and colors, but the details elude us. We see things from a limited, finite perspective.

If we try to see things from a different perspective—trying on someone else's lenses for a while—things look blurry and feel awkward at first. But the longer we leave on the new glasses, the more our eyes will naturally adjust. Eventually we may adapt so well that we forget we ever saw things in any other way. It's possible to change our vision, but the process isn't always comfortable.

What lenses do you wear when you are listening to your children? Have you ever considered borrowing their specs for a time? Your children see the same things that you see, but their perspective is different. If you are going to help your children develop a worldview that corresponds to "ultimate reality," you've got to know how they're seeing things now. We pray that our children's worldview will have God as its central point of reference.

How we view the world matters for us—as Christians and as parents. It governs the way that we live, and it determines what we will model for those who look to us for guidance. Obviously, we can't choose our worldview in the way that we choose our shoes. Carefully considering the questions that a worldview answers takes time and serious thought, but the effort is well worth the energy we put into it. Hitler's worldview led him to kill millions of innocent people. Mother Teresa's worldview, on the other hand, led her to minister to hurting people the rest of the world had forgotten. Both Hitler and Mother Teresa had passion, but their worldviews made all the difference.

A worldview that we feel passionate about and can articulate well will decisively affect our parenting, especially if it connects our hearts with eternity (Ecclesiastes 3:11). Such a worldview comprehends an ultimate authority that has instilled spiritual hunger in the hearts of men, women, and children. It gives us a deep-seated belief that there is more to life than what we see and that God is in control (2 Corinthians 4:17-18). It is predetermined, never-changing, higher spiritual truth. We must spend time in learning to articulate our worldview and its relevance to our children, but as we watch God work in them, we may discover something valuable in their worldviews as well.

Chapter 5
Ultimate Reality or Virtual Reality?

If you've ever had someone you've never met pick you up at the airport, you know what a strange experience it can be. Normally, you can tell who it is because the person is standing there nervously scanning the people coming off the plane. Finally there is that moment of recognition: "Is it you? Yes? Great!"

Os Guinness tells of a time when the person who was supposed to pick him up didn't step forward until several awkward minutes had gone by. The person's statement was priceless. "I'm so sorry," he said. "I completely missed you. I was expecting someone quite different."[1] How do you respond to that?

We all carry preconceived ideas of what people will look like before we meet them. When you first meet someone in person whom you've only spoken with on the phone, how often do you come away saying something like, "He's not as tall as I thought he'd be"? Where do we get these ideas about how tall someone should be? Why are we surprised when the person we meet doesn't look like their voice sounds or sound like their picture looks? We are remarkably unreliable when we fill gaps in our knowledge with our own ideas of how things ought to be.

Suppose that the person at the airport had refused to change his predetermined idea of what Os Guinness should look like. He would have believed that Guinness had never arrived at the airport. In one sense, he would have been right. Os Guinness, as he existed in this man's mind, never showed up because *there is no such Os Guinness.*

Our preconceived ideas about God work in much the same way.

Our minds paint pictures of a God who is other than God as he really is. It's possible for us to go through life believing that God has not shown up because what we "see" doesn't fit our preconceptions; or we hope he won't show up because we don't want to meet him as we think he is.

"What comes into our minds when we think about God," A. W. Tozer said, "is the most important thing about us."[2] Our concept of God determines how we feel, think, and act toward him. If we believe that God is a celestial Santa Claus, we had better watch out and not cry or pout if we want something special in our Christmas stocking. If we think God is a cosmic killjoy, we will always be waiting for the other shoe to drop, certain that it's only a matter of time before we get zapped for having too much fun. Our idea of God may resemble an absentminded grandfather, a step-and-fetch-it butler, or a heavenly vending machine. What we believe about God sets up the dominoes that will fall during the course of our lifetime.

If you raise your kids to think that God is a harsh, law-giving taskmaster, ready to squash them when they cross the line, then their lives will be full of anxiety. Their lives will be one long series of backflips and handstands they perform in an effort to gain the approval of an impossible-to-please tyrant.

If you raise your kids to believe that God is distant and unconcerned, they will probably grow up saying, "I don't care what he thinks of me or my life. I'll live anyway I please. Why should I care about him if he doesn't care about me?"

If your child grows up knowing that God is merciful, forgiving, patient, and faithful . . . that changes everything. The entire world is dying to hear that such a love is possible. Your children need to know that this love characterizes the God of your faith. Children will get their initial impressions of who God is and what he is like from their parents— from their dads in particular. Think about that the next time your kid spills her milk on you at the dinner table.

All ideas have consequences, and when pressed to their logical conclusions, ours will either affirm or deny God as he actually exists. Our ideas will cause us either to embrace or reject a lifestyle that honors him. They have the potential to lead us into a life that alienates us from him or one that motivates us to seek his protection.

Everything begins and ends with God. If our children believe that God exists, that he is active in their lives, and that he loves them dearly, more than half of the battle is already won.

WE'VE FALLEN AND WE CAN'T GET UP

It is difficult to have an accurate view of God. In fact, it is impossible in our own power because we are all fallen creatures and we cannot help ourselves. The effects of sin have damaged every part of us—our bodies, our relationships, and our minds. If anyone has ever told you that there's something wrong with your mind, they're telling you the truth. Your mind was affected by the Fall—our inaccurate views of God can be traced back to our ancestors' sin in the Garden.

Because we are finite and imperfect, the only hope we have of gaining an accurate vision of God is for him to reveal himself to us. The Bible tells us that we cannot see God (John 1:18; 1 Timothy 6:16) or discover him on our own (Job 11:7; 23:3-9). The Bible also says that we're kidding ourselves if we think that we can read God's mind, guess his motives, or predict his actions by our own unaided reason, because his thoughts are not our thoughts (Isaiah 55:8-9).

In the previous chapter, we talked about differences between dogs and people. Compared to humans, dogs have very limited and different mental abilities. A dog can only handle and process a small amount of information, in human terms. A human's capacity for processing information is also limited, but humans are capable of storing and processing a great deal more than dogs are.

There is some overlap between the mental faculties of dogs and humans. Dogs and humans both understand food, but dogs can't cook. When a human stares at pieces of paper and slowly turns the pages of a book, a dog doesn't get it. A dog has no capacity for reading. We have dogs as pets because there is enough common ground between us for limited communication ("Fetch!"), and a human can teach a pet certain things ("Shake!"). Few people keep worms or butterflies as pets because so little communication is possible with them.

There is enough overlap between humans and dogs for a human to love a dog without condescension. We don't despise a dog for being unable to understand geometry. That would be ridiculous! We understand that dogs have limited mental abilities by virtue of what they are. We don't fault them when they can fetch the morning paper but aren't able to read it.

God is infinitely more different from humans than humans are from dogs. Humans have a greater mental capacity than dogs, but it is still finite. God's capacity is boundless, yet God can communicate with us and we can communicate with him. This communication is limited by our human capacities but is nonetheless real.

God's divine love creates a person's desire to seek him and know him as he has revealed himself. This is called *prevenient grace*. Watch your children for very long, and you will understand that they seek God. They may not know it is God they are seeking, but we are all born for this. We all have a sense of how things are supposed to be, and we know that we are not meant to be alienated and alone. We sense this deep within our bones. There is a residue of heaven—God's fingerprints—on every child. We seek God because he is seeking us. From the moment of our birth, God begins to draw us to himself. He has placed within each of us the hunger to find him.

This is where the spiritual life of children begins. Each of them is born into a quest, a search for transcendence and wonder, a hunt for God. We all come into this world running in two directions at once—running away from God and at the same time desperately trying to find him. We and our children are likely to end up at one of three destinations.

HUNGERING FOR THE WRONG GOD

Humans are finite and sinful creatures with an amazing capacity for suppressing and distorting the revelation God has given us of himself. We hunger for God, but we try to satisfy this longing with cheap substitutes. We look for meaning and fulfillment in possessions and activities, hoping these things will slake our insatiable thirst for transcendence. Very early, children begin to define themselves and others by what they own and do.

"I'm a soccer player."

"You're that loser who failed second grade."

"She's that girl who drives a Lexus."

Labels dominate our lives from our earliest stages, reinforcing the need to fill the vacuum in our hearts with material things and accomplishments. Unfortunately, this approach is as deadly as drinking saltwater. When we set our anchors in anything other than the bedrock of God's true character, we are guilty of idolatry, and idolatry always leads to death.

The Ten Commandments are among the best-known passages of Scripture. Each commandment provides a deep spiritual truth that can help us to know God and how he wants us to live. In the second commandment, God says, "You shall not make for yourself an idol in the form of anything in heaven above or on the earth beneath or in the waters below. You shall not bow down to them or worship them" (Exodus 20:4-5). An idol is something that people make to represent God. Sometimes idols are statues that people bow down to and worship as if they really represented God.

As parents, we may sincerely believe that we are not guilty of idolatry. After all, we're Christians, right? And yet if we are honest, we have to say that we have bowed down to idols. There are idols of busyness, status, approval, and intellectual superiority. An idol is really anything that becomes more important to us than God. Regardless of our idol of choice, the result is the same: death. That death may come quickly, or it may be more like a slowly progressing terminal illness—exhaustion or crushing debt that allows the life to ebb out of us almost unnoticed. Often we are lifeless because the wrong God reigns in our minds.

We say that we want to lead simple, God-honoring lives, and on some level that's true. But there are other things that we want more, or we wouldn't be living as we are. In a 1999 national survey, George Barna found that the percentage of born-again Christians who had experienced divorce was actually higher than that of non-Christians (26 percent compared to 22 percent).[3] This number has remained relatively consistent since the mid-1990s. In August 2001, a new poll found that the divorce rate among Christians had dipped slightly below that of non-Christian Americans, but the rate had gone up from 26 percent to 33 percent (compared to 34 percent for non-Christians, a statistically insignificant difference). Perhaps the worst statistical finding regarding divorce and Christians in America is that 90 percent of divorced Christians divorced *after* they accepted Christ.[4]

Divorce is not the church's only black eye. American Christians live in the wealthiest nation on the planet, enjoying an average household income of $42,409.[5] The World Bank reports that more than a billion of the world's poorest people survive on just one dollar a day. Nearly that many have never heard the good news of Jesus. If American Christians gave 10 percent of their income, we would have more than $140 billion available to work against poverty and spread the gospel.[6] Studies by the United Nations suggest that half that amount would provide access to basic health care and education for all the impoverished peoples on earth.[7]

We claim that the Bible is our final authority, but one of the most common themes throughout the Bible is God's concern for poor and marginalized people in society. It is becoming increasingly obvious that our walk does not match our talk in the way that we care for oppressed people in our world.

Racism is another area of concern. In 1989, George Gallup Jr. and James Castelli published the results of a survey that examined which groups in America were least likely and most likely to object to having African-American neighbors. Catholics and nonevangelical Christians ranked least likely to object (11 percent). Mainline Protestants came next at 16 percent. Among the groups most likely to object to black neighbors were Baptists and evangelicals at 17 percent. Southern Baptists were even more likely to object (20 percent).[8]

Michael O. Emerson and Christian Smith have written a book exploring ongoing racial attitudes in the evangelical world. They conclude that "white evangelicalism likely does more to perpetuate the racialized society than to reduce it."[9] Conservative white Protestants are more than twice as likely as other whites to blame lack of economic equality among the races on laziness and lack of motivation. Conservative Protestants are six times more likely to cite lack of motivation than unequal access to quality education.[10]

Good biblical ecclesiology tells us that in the church racial distinctions should not matter, but if this theology is not applied in our neighborhoods, schools, and workplaces, racist structures will endure. We must not allow a disconnection between what we claim in our statements of belief and who we actually are. Our children are learning from us what a mature adult follower of Christ looks like. *As we honestly examine our faith, perhaps we will find that we suffer less from lack of faith than from faith in the wrong deity—the deity of self, comfort, or the status quo.*

If you want to know whether you have the wrong god, think back to a time of crisis. To what or whom did you turn in that moment? Our real picture of God isn't established by what we say we believe, but by what we rely upon when the heat is turned up. That is also what our children will remember. If we tell our children that God is the trustworthy source of every material blessing, but we work eighty hours a week, kick the dog when the stock market dips, or panic like Chicken Little when the car starts making funny noises, they're going to realize that our faith is more talk than walk. At some point, it may be necessary for us to admit that we doubt the true God and believe wholeheartedly in the wrong god.

Our problem may be that there is no such god as the one that exists in our minds.

RIGHT GOD . . . KIND OF

Maybe we don't have the wrong god. It could be that our God-perception is just somewhat off the mark. When Jesus walked in Israel some two thousand years ago, people often came to him with some idea of who he was, but few came with a complete understanding. They were on the right track, but they hadn't gone far enough.

Two examples help us to see this. First, a man with leprosy came to Jesus asking for help. "You have the power to make me well, if only you wanted to" (Mark 1:40, CEV). Translation: "You could do it if you wanted to, but you probably don't want to." This guy understood Jesus' power over disease, but he was way off track about Jesus' heart.

Second, a father whose son was being tormented by a demon came to Jesus asking for help. "If you can do anything, take pity on us and help us" (Mark 9:22). Translation: "I know you would if you could, but you probably can't." This guy had a sense of Jesus' compassionate heart, but he had no concept of his power.

Sometimes, in trying to make God accessible to our children, we shrink him down until he's just a little bit bigger than we are. At other times, we swing the pendulum too far in the opposite direction, giving our kids the impression that God is so powerful that he can do anything he wants—even if he decides on a whim to squash them like a bug or change his mind about the whole heaven thing—and no one can say a word to him about it.

A man who has worked at Christian summer camps for years told us that at least once every summer he has a conversation with a teen who says, "I can't know for sure if I'm saved because God could change his mind at any time. After all, he's God." We're not exactly sure who that teen is talking about, but it's not God.

IS GOD SAFE?

When we invent a god to suit our tastes or alter the picture God reveals of himself in the Bible, we end up with a god no one really wants. Who needs a god who is tame, predictable, and easy to manipulate? Who wants a god who is either all "forgive and forget" or all judgment? When the road narrows and the light grows dim, such a god simply will not do. A false image of God results in a false relationship with a false god.

It is difficult to find a both/and description of God. As parents, you know that most children's literature presents an either/or description. A children's Bible may present a flannel-board Jesus who resembles Mr. Rogers more than the roaring Lion of Judah.[11] Reactionary authors seem determined to inform children that hell is hot, eternity is long, and God punishes the wicked by pouring out his unlimited wrath on them. Whatever you may think of that theology, it's probably inappropriate bedtime reading for the average six-year-old.

Why doesn't God make it clear? Why doesn't he just come down and let everyone know who he is and what he's like? Well, he did exactly that. The fullest, most accurate picture of God is found in Jesus. You can get an idea of God's character by looking at the beautiful world he created. You can get a sense of his majesty by listening to an orchestra or watching the sun set over the Kansas plains. You can feel his playfulness and mystery when you see a litter of newborn puppies, and you can understand something of his nature when you meditate on noble thoughts and work toward justice among the poor and oppressed. But God decided that the best way to reveal himself to humans was to become human. Jesus was God in human form.[12]

So how can we help our kids to get a picture of God as he really exists? A child will not be able to understand Jesus thoroughly, any more than adults can. One excellent way to share the real God with children is to read to them. It will instill in them a lifelong love of reading, provide many teachable moments, and build your relationship by enabling you to enter other conceptual and imaginative worlds together. Watching movies (carefully chosen) with your child can provide another such venue for exploring God's character.

Two theologically rich stories from the Chronicles of Narnia by C. S. Lewis provide us with good illustrations of God's character. In the first and best-known book of this series, *The Lion, the Witch, and the Wardrobe,* the lion named Aslan is a Christ figure. In one passage, the characters Mr. and Mrs. Beaver are about to introduce Peter, Susan, Edmund, and Lucy to Aslan. As the Beavers describe him, however, the children are not quite sure that they want to meet him after all. Mr. Beaver says to them:

"Wrong will be right, when Aslan comes in sight.

At the sound of his roar, sorrows will be no more.

When he bares his teeth, winter meets its death.

And when he shakes his mane, we shall have spring again.

You'll understand when you see him."

"But shall we see him?" asked Susan.

"Why, Daughter of Eve, that's what I brought you here for. I'm to lead you where you shall meet him," said Mr. Beaver.

"Is—is he a man?" asked Lucy.

"Aslan a man!" said Mr. Beaver sternly. "Certainly not. I tell you he is the King of the wood and the son of the great Emperor-Beyond-the-Sea. Don't you know who is the King of Beasts? Aslan is a lion—THE Lion, the great Lion."

"Ooh!" said Susan. "I'd thought he was a man. Is he—quite safe? I shall feel rather nervous about meeting a lion."

"That you will dearie, and no mistake," said Mrs. Beaver, "if anyone can appear before Aslan without their knees knocking, they are either braver than most or else just silly."

"Then he isn't safe?" said Lucy.

"Safe?" said Mr. Beaver. "Don't you hear what Mrs. Beaver tells you? Who said anything about safe? Course he isn't safe. But he's good. He's the King, I tell you."[13]

Is Jesus safe? Not by a long shot. Consider his own words:

I have come to bring fire on the earth, and how I wish it were already kindled! But I have a baptism to undergo, and how distressed I am until it is completed! Do you think I came to bring peace on earth? No, I tell you, but division. From now on there will be five in one family divided against each other, three against two and two against three. They will be divided, father against son and son against father, mother against daughter and daughter against mother, mother-in-law against daughter-in-law and daughter-in-law against mother-in-law. (Luke 12:49-53)

These are not very comforting words—especially for parents! Is Jesus safe? He was kind and gentle. He invited children to come near, and he blessed them. He cried when a friend died. He helped people who were ill and had compassion on those who were brokenhearted and distressed. That seems safe.

And yet there are other stories that show a darker side to Jesus. He had to run from people who threatened to kill him. The Prince of Peace, who came to bring God's shalom to earth and who longs to reconcile us to the Father and with one another, is the cause of many divisions. Because of him, parents and children are often divided, battles are fought, and wars are waged. Safe? Who said anything about safe?

As it turns out, the only thing more dangerous than having an inaccurate picture of God is having an accurate one. Jesus is not always nice. He isn't the kind of guy who sits quietly and avoids rocking the boat. If someone came to your church promising to bring fire and division and to get everyone worked up, you'd probably say, "We fired the last guy for that." Who needs that kind of hassle?

Jesus shook people up—often when they least expected it. The rich lawyer who wanted to justify himself was devastated when Jesus looked him in the eye and told him to sell everything he had and give it to the poor. By unmasking the lawyer's priorities, Jesus enabled him to see where his heart was, and it wasn't in sharing his wealth with others.

When Jesus sat down to dinner with tax collectors, prostitutes, and other disreputable people, even the disciples were taken aback. "These aren't respectable people, Jesus. They're not the kind of nice folks you'd want to take home to meet your mother. Jesus, what in the world are you doing? Don't you know who they are?" Jesus unmasked the disciples' deep prejudices and made them rethink their lack of love toward the very ones for whom God cares. He said to them, "Of course I know who they are. Don't you know who I am?"

Jesus often said things that people didn't like. That's one reason they killed him. His ministry was bathed in blood, and the blood of martyrs still follows him. He did not come to lead the ladies' tea or the men's golf outing. A lot of times what he said couldn't be repeated in polite company. His message was controversial, and it still is. We only have to think of recent elections to see that both sides of the political spectrum can quote Jesus' words to equally divisive effect. God's people in America can't even agree on the core message of Christianity.

Jesus did not come to make us feel good about our motives or our behavior. He did not come to bless our complacency, affirm our respectability, or confirm our sentimental notions of traditional family values. He came to show us a better way to live, to care for others, and to live in relationship with God and his promises. It's that simple and that difficult.

Jesus confronts us with a picture of a God who disturbs our peace in order to bring his purposes to birth in our hearts. God cuts through the facades of our lives to reveal our true loyalties and commitments. Such truth does not often bring people closer together. It rarely builds consensus or brings peace as we normally understand it. Truth often reveals pain; it is divisive because it exposes our lies, hypocrisy, and self-centeredness. Truth makes us struggle with our faith as we realize that issues such as abortion, capital punishment, and poverty are not easily swept aside. We need this struggle if we are to be healed and become the people that God calls us to be. We already know much of the answer to division and apathy, but it's an answer we don't particularly like. After talking about division and swords, Jesus talked about his death. The only peace we get is in his death, which erases the divisions that separate us. We can no longer hide behind our respectability, status, wealth, or self-importance. To be faithful, we must put to death our high opinions of ourselves, our preoccupation with our own comfort and respectability, and our tendency to see ourselves as masters of our own domains rather than as participants and agents for peace in the whole human community.

We must let go of those things that do not bring us God's peace. We must accept responsibility for hurting one another, ask for forgiveness, and work for healing. We must banish the things that do not express God's loving intent, and we must allow God to strip them of their power to control our choices.

Safe? Who said anything about safe? What we find in Jesus is a God who loves us infinitely and will not let us go—a God who disturbs our self-made peace.

Another story from the Chronicles of Narnia is less well known but equally instructive. In *The Silver Chair,* a conceited girl named Jill Pole lands in Narnia with Eustace Scrubb, a formerly bratty child who in an earlier visit to Narnia endured an excruciating but transforming encounter with Aslan the Lion. Jill gets into a tussle with Eustace at a cliff's edge and pushes him off. As Eustace falls, Aslan blows a huge stream of breath to catch Eustace and carry him far away to safety—and to danger of another sort (but that's another story).

Aslan turns and—much to Jill's relief—walks back into the forest.

Jill grows unbearably thirsty. She can hear a stream somewhere in the forest. Driven by her thirst, she begins to look for this source of water— cautiously, because she is fearful of running into the Lion. She finds the stream, but she is paralyzed by what she sees there: Aslan, huge and golden, still as a statue but terribly alive, is sitting beside the water. She waits for a long time, wrestling with her thoughts and hoping that he'll just go away.

Then Aslan says, "If you are thirsty, you may drink."

Jill is startled and refuses to come closer.

> "Are you not thirsty?" said the Lion.
>
> "I am *dying* of thirst," said Jill.
>
> "Then drink," said the Lion.
>
> "May I—could I—would you mind going away while I do?" said Jill.
>
> The Lion answered this only by a look and a very low growl. And just as Jill gazed at its motionless bulk, she realized that she might as well have asked the whole mountain to move aside for her convenience.
>
> The delicious rippling noise of the stream was driving her near frantic.
>
> "Will you promise not to—do anything to me, if I come?"

"I make no promise," said the Lion.

Jill was so thirsty now that, without noticing it, she had come a step nearer.

"Do you eat girls?" she said.

"I have swallowed up girls and boys, women and men, kings and emperors, cities and realms," said the Lion. It didn't say this as if it were boasting, nor as if it were sorry, nor as if it were angry. It just said it.

"I daren't come and drink," said Jill.

"Then you will die of thirst," said the Lion.

"Oh dear!" said Jill, coming another step nearer. "I suppose I must go and look for another stream then."

"There is no other stream," said the Lion.[14]

God doesn't give us many options. There is no other stream. We drink from this one or we die.

DEFINING REALITY

God is the absolute arbiter of that which is good, true, and beautiful. He will never abdicate his position as sovereign Lord of all that was, is, and ever shall be. He will not be tamed, sanitized, or sent away, and he alone defines reality. Any attempts on our part to reframe what he has said results in temporary discomfort and eternal loss.

If you went to a casino, rolled the dice and got snake eyes, you might be disappointed, but not surprised. If you rolled the dice again and got a pair of twos, you might not give it a second thought. But if you rolled a third time and got two threes, you'd probably wonder about the odds of something like that happening. If you rolled again and got fours, then a pair of fives, and then sixes, you'd begin asking questions.

If you kept on rolling those dice all day long and got the same sequence—a pair of ones, then twos, threes, and so on, eventually you'd stop and say, "This can't be chance. Someone's playing a trick here, or these dice are loaded, or something's not right." Random chance goes only so far.

For centuries, people have looked at the complexities of our universe and said the same thing. "This can't happen by chance. Random chance only goes so far." This commonsense line of reasoning went basically unchallenged until what is ironically referred to as the Age of Reason, when otherwise reasonable scientists began postulating that the universe might be the result of random chance plus time.

It's not too likely that a fully assembled airplane will result when a steel mill explodes, no matter how many times it happens. The mathematical probability that a chance collision of floating gases will eventually produce a single living microorganism, let alone a process as complex as photosynthesis or a dolphin swimming, is so highly unlikely as to be unreasonable. When you consider the physiological wonder of your children's existence—her ears, eyes, and skin, his sense of touch and smell, their emotional and mental capacities—it takes a lot more faith to believe that these resulted from a gaseous explosion billions of years ago than to believe that we were custom-designed by an intentional God. And it is this God who makes the rules.

This is offensive to some, but couched in the reality of God's identity, it only makes sense. What are the rules according to God? That's what we're going to look at next. But before we do, put down this book, go find your kids, and just look at them. They might squirm and wiggle, but look at them anyway. Marvel once more at how fearfully and wonderfully God has made them. Then *tell them* how marvelous they are. Cellist Pablo Casals asked people to tell their children the following things:

> You are a marvel.
>
> You are unique.
>
> In all the years that have passed, there has never been another child like you.
>
> Your legs, your arms, your clever fingers, the way you move.
>
> You may become a Shakespeare, a Michelangelo, a Beethoven.
>
> You have the capacity for anything.[15]

Then tell your children how their amazing design points beyond themselves to a God who knows exactly what he's doing, a God whom they can trust completely both now and in the future when they think that no one understands them. Then come back to this book, and we'll move on.

Until now we have been discussing weighty issues in general language. But all of this philosophical thinking can leave parents scratching their heads. How does a parent explain all of this to a child? And what, specifically, should parents communicate?

We are not going to present you with a one-size-fits-all, cookie-cutter approach to what you ought to teach your children. However, we believe that there are some universal, irreducible minimums that all children need to know if they are going to begin assembling a view of the world that corresponds to historic orthodox Christianity.

We will summarize some basic responses to the great fundamental questions of meaning, purpose, and destiny. To make them easy to remember, we'll use the five *W*s—*who, what, where, when,* and *why.*

WHO AM I?

Society had scarcely put in place the infrastructure needed to support the technological advances of the past decade when a new kind of crime sprang up: identity theft. People who are victims of this crime spend months, even years, cleaning up the mess left by the perpetrators. It's impossible to estimate the number of people affected, the millions of dollars lost, or the time and emotional energy spent in restoring reputations damaged when someone wrongfully obtains and uses another person's personal data for fraud or deception, most typically for financial gain. Victims often feel especially violated because not only was this crime committed *against* them, but—in the eyes of many unsuspecting merchants—

it was committed *by* them. Identity theft is psychologically damaging because it affects who others believe you are.

We think that we would never allow someone we didn't know to define us, and yet we are bombarded by messages from the media that attempt to do this very thing. Perhaps you've never thought of it this way, but some of the smartest people on the planet are paid by some of the wealthiest people to stay up late figuring out how to convince you that if you do not buy their product, there is something wrong with you. No wonder some children and teenagers go through an acute identity crisis!

A Christian worldview can help. Once we realize that it is reasonable to believe in God's existence and that the Bible is God's self-revelation, we can turn to his Word for wisdom regarding our true identity. Its assessment of our lives is refreshingly honest. The Bible affirms our unique status as humans while also pinpointing our frustrating inadequacies. It defines our innate potential and challenges us to improve. How can we make these ideas kid friendly? Let's summarize them in simple terms.

Who am I? I am a treasure created in God's image. That means that God made me and loves me just as I am. But if that were the whole story, Jesus would not have had to come to earth. I am also a sinner unable to save myself. I do not just happen to sin; I sin because I am a sinner. There is something wrong with me that I can't fix, no matter how hard I try.

God is not content to leave me broken. By his grace, he offers to accept my trust in place of perfection. Once I place my trust in him, he considers me a saint even when I don't act like one. My failures can never end my relationship with him.

God is also going to help me to live in freedom with purpose and significance. He offers me a new kind of life that doesn't just get me into heaven when I die, but makes a difference here and now. He wants me to be a follower and friend of Jesus. I can help bring about God's kingdom on earth by spreading light in a dark world, by bringing a spot of color to a black-and-white landscape.

Bob and Jenn Nahrstadt are lay leaders in their church just outside of Chicago. When we asked them how they would answer if their child asked, "Who am I?" Bob's response was so good that we wanted to share it with you. Bob tells his son that he is God's very own personal Lego Millennium Falcon spaceship. Here's the story in Bob's words:

> To understand this, you have to know that for his tenth birthday our son received a gazillion-piece Lego Star Wars Millennium Falcon spaceship kit. He spent hours with his mom putting it together. It was his pride and joy—his very own creation! He loved his Millennium Falcon. But then the unthinkable happened: The Millennium Falcon fell off the dining room table, shattering into hundreds of tiny pieces!
>
> The thing he loved so much was broken, and he cried with the kind of broken heart you can only have as a ten-year-old boy. He cried the tears of a creator who has just seen his masterpiece broken into bits.
>
> But even as he was crying, he sat down on the floor and gathered up all the pieces. Still wiping tears, he began the painstakingly slow process of putting it all back together again. He didn't leave the Millennium Falcon broken on the floor. He loved it too much for that. He wanted to go on enjoying it. A year later, he still plays with that rebuilt Millennium Falcon.
>
> So, if I told my son that he is God's Millennium Falcon, he would understand that God created him and loved him. He would also understand how, when sin entered the world, he became broken and how this hurt God's heart. He would understand a little of how God feels about sin and the destruction it inevitably brings. He would understand that God still wants to spend time with him and enjoy him, so he sent Jesus to repair what's broken and put him back together again.
>
> The analogy may not be theologically complete (my son did not die for his Legos), but he is only ten. Maybe he will catch enough of who he is through this simple comparison to his own experience.

Deuteronomy 11 says, "Love the LORD your God and keep his requirements, his decrees, his laws and his commands always. Remember today that your children were not the ones who saw and experienced the discipline of the LORD your God: his majesty, his mighty hand, his outstretched arm; the signs he performed and the things he did in the heart of Egypt. . . . It was your own eyes that saw all these great things the LORD has done.

"Fix these words of mine in your hearts and minds; tie them as symbols on your hands and bind them on your foreheads. Teach them to your children, talking about them when you sit at home and when you walk along the road, when you lie down and when you get up. Write them on the doorframes of your houses and on your gates, so that your days and the days of your children may be many in the land that the LORD swore to give your forefathers" (Deuteronomy 11:1-3, 7, 18-21).[1]

Bob and Jenn looked for opportunities to communicate their faith in God to their son. They made a connection between something their son truly loved and the One who truly loves their son. Once you start looking for these teachable moments, you'll be surprised at how often they come up.

WHAT IS CHRISTIANITY?

Perhaps no other question gets as many different answers as this one. To some, Christianity is a marketing tool that gets people to do what other people want them to do. Some believe Christianity is the reason for the good that is in the world, whereas others think it is responsible for evil. For some, it has to do with going to church, maintaining a family identity, or keeping a list of things that we avoid.

Christianity is none of those things. To put it in "kidspeak," Christianity is God's plan to get all his lost kids home again. Christianity is the crazy idea that God is using all the good and bad stuff that happens to us to make us more and more like Jesus. Christianity means living as if God really is doing this. Christians have found this really great leader named Jesus and follow him wherever he goes, doing what he does in the way that he does it.

Once Jesus was asked to sum up what a God-honoring life looks like. He said, "'Love the Lord your God with all your heart and with all your soul and with all your mind.' This is the first and greatest commandment. And the second is like it: 'Love your neighbor as yourself.' All the Law and the Prophets hang on these two commandments" (Matthew 22:37-40).

A follower of Jesus loves God and loves other people for the good of the whole world. This means subscribing to a clearly defined set of actions, beliefs, and virtues. We give God our minds, bodies, and hearts to use as he sees fit. For the early Pietist Christians, "the true criteria of authentic Christianity were orthopathy (right feelings) and orthopraxy (right living) along with orthodoxy (right believing)." They also argued that "right experience and right living would inevitably lead to right believing."[2]

Christianity is more than a set of beliefs to which a person assents. In the words of Kurt Bruner, it is "a worldview sophisticated enough to encompass every academic discipline and resolve life's thorniest problems, while simple enough to prompt a tiny child to sing, 'Jesus loves me this I know, for the Bible tells me so.'"[3] It is thus appropriate to search the Bible for those actions, beliefs, and virtues that will enable us to love God and others for everyone's good.

For centuries, Christians have read the Bible and compiled a list of its overarching themes. Systematic theology is the practice of taking the most significant and commonly recurring themes of the Bible and putting each into a separate category for comprehensive examination. Studying these themes teaches us how to think and live in a Christian way. These core beliefs teach us who God is, how we are invited to enter into relationship with him, what he wants us to know and do, how he is involved in our lives, and who we become when we know and surrender to God.

Just believing that these are the right answers is not sufficient. The point is not just to exchange information. The goal is to renew our minds. As people who have chosen to follow Jesus, we allow our thinking to be saturated with the truth of God's Word so that it forms and informs the way we live and how we understand our world.

A Christian society is made up of Christian individuals, Christian businesses, and Christian households. Can a household be called a Christian home if its people are ignorant of Christianity's core beliefs about loving God and others? Perhaps the cultural revival that church leaders have anticipated will be realized when families are committed to growing "in the grace and knowledge of our Lord and Savior Jesus Christ" (2 Peter 3:18).

Through the centuries, Christians have realized that certain disciplines are essential for spiritual health. They do not guarantee a person's spiritual maturity, but they help a person to become mature by providing opportunities for the Spirit of God to work. These practices include prayer, Bible study, meditation, gratitude, and generosity, among others. Think of what might happen in a family committed to practicing these behaviors.

Beliefs involve what we need to know, practices concern what we need to do, and virtues point to what we need to be. Through the work of the Holy Spirit, God wants us to develop virtues that express what it means to be like Jesus. Joy, courage, humility, and determination are some of the qualities inherent in the normal lifestyle of those who have surrendered heart, mind, and body to God.

Our behavior reinforces our beliefs. As our beliefs are shaped, virtues are forged in our hearts, and they seek expression through specific behaviors. Christianity, like good parenting, is not just behavior modification or a collection of correct doctrines or rules. Plenty of people are "high pagans"; they hold Christian values but do not regard themselves as Christians. Christians modify their behavior, hold correct doctrine, and forge certain values *because* they love God and other people for the good of the world.

WHERE IS GOD AT WORK?

God is everywhere. He blows in the wind and swims with the fish. He is in the earth and beyond the moon. He is in the sun and inside of your skin. He is closer than you think and farther than you can imagine—even if you have a great imagination! You can't run to a place where God is not, and you can never find all of him. He is the God of the vast realms of outer space and the God of the tiniest molecules of inner space.

God has chosen to limit the way that he works in our world. He is able to work through any means, but for the most part he works through three institutions: the family, the church, and the government. Christians live in families, they are members of a body of believers, and they are citizens of a particular region.

Families are the primary building blocks of society. If something goes wrong in a society, look at the families in that society to find out why. If you want to fix cultural problems, don't start with the schools, start with the families. We are all born into families and raised in them. Some families are broken through divorce, abandonment, and abuse, but every family is broken in some way because sin has infiltrated every individual, and thus every home. This is why parenting is such a world-changing task. To paraphrase Russell Crowe's line from the movie *Gladiator*: The things we do as parents will echo throughout eternity.

This also means that when we depart from the Bible's original plan for families, things get messy. God designed the home to function with a man and a woman who are in a deeply committed relationship to God and to one another. Into this home, children are born. There are many alternatives to this biblical ideal, and there are many problems as a result.

Maggie Gallagher, coauthor of *The Case for Marriage: Why Married People Are Happier, Healthier, and Better-Off Financially,* says it bluntly: "Children raised by their own mothers and fathers in a married home do better than those who are not."[4] According to Gallagher's research, children raised in single-parent homes are more likely to experience deep and persistent poverty, be held back at school, suffer physical and mental health problems, become victims of child abuse, become involved in juvenile delinquency and substance abuse, and suffer from behavioral disorders. As adults, they are less likely to earn good incomes, keep their jobs, or have their own children within the context of marriage. "Children raised outside of marriage are at substantially increased risk for just about every negative outcome that social scientists can measure," Gallagher said in testimony before the Massachusetts state legislature.[5]

These statistics are not meant to disparage the efforts of single parents. However, they show that overall, marriage is important for children and for society. As parents committed to spreading God's agenda in our world, we have a real opportunity to make a difference by setting our own households in order. Strengthening our own marriages and those of the people in our churches may be the single most significant thing we can do to improve the moral environment of our culture.

The next institution God established for accomplishing his purposes is a community of people who gather together to encourage one another and hold each other accountable for living the gospel. In our time, that community of people is known as the church. Regardless of our political leanings, we can probably all agree that if the church took seriously its responsibility to be the light in a dark world, to be the hands and feet of Jesus, and to extend compassion, acceptance, and benevolence to widows, orphans, and foreigners, the government would have to downsize considerably. It is largely because the American church in the twentieth century has failed to do these things that the government has stepped in with such extensive social programs.

But this book is about parenting, not political science. Specifically, we are concerned with living in such a way that our children learn to view the world through a biblical lens. We will therefore limit our discussion of the church as God's divinely ordained institution to how it affects our ability to live in God-honoring and child-formative ways.

We must concern ourselves, for example, with the impact that church attendance has on children. A 2001 study conducted by the Barna Research Group discovered that those who attended church regularly as a child were nearly three times as likely to attend church in adulthood as their peers who avoided church during childhood (60 percent compared to 22 percent). Nearly two-thirds of those who attended church as children take their own children to church (63 percent), which is almost double the number of unchurched adults who take their kids to church (33 percent). Adults who attended church as a child are nearly 50 percent more likely to pray to God during a typical week than those who did not attend church as children.[6]

In a 2003 study, Barna discovered that nearly all parents (96 percent) believe that they have the primary responsibility for teaching values to their children, but most of them don't know how to do this. The most incredible statistics are these: In a typical weekend, 37 percent of single adults and 53 percent of married people in the United States attend church; however, about two out of three parents of children twelve or younger attend religious services at least once a month and generally take their children with them.

Parents obviously know the importance of teaching values to their children. Often they just don't have a plan, have little or no training in nurturing a child's faith, or have no experience or accountability. And yet they go to church weekend after weekend. What are they looking for?

And how does the typical church respond? "Mr. and Mrs. Jones, welcome. We want you to know that at Grace Community Church, we are family-friendly. In fact, we have a staff of trained volunteers who will provide child care while you enjoy the fellowship and instruction of our adult Bible-class teachers and worship leaders. You won't have to give your kids a second thought. Just let us take care of them for you."

Research suggests that one of the primary reasons parents are coming to church is that they are looking for help in raising their children. And that's the one thing churches don't want them to think about? Churches spend a lot of time ministering to parents as adults, but they spend very little time ministering to adults as parents. Barna's survey found that only one out of every five parents of children under thirteen (19 percent) had ever been personally contacted by a church leader to discuss the parents' involvement in the spiritual life and development of their children.

As one of three divinely ordained institutions, the church has to do better than that!

God established the family at the time of Creation. He began establishing his community of people with his promise to Abraham (Genesis 12) and continued doing so until the outpouring of his Holy Spirit at the formation of the church (Acts 2). God established a third institution in civil government. Theologians have debated for centuries over when exactly that happened, but government was probably a *creation ordinance* (an institution that God established forever at creation). Had sin never entered the world, people would still have needed roads and standards of fair trade, such as weights and measures.

Each of these three institutions has its own realm of operation. God has vested each with his authority, and all three are directly accountable to him. This is a foreign idea to some. In totalitarian states, for example, every area of society is subject to one dominant institution, which is usually the state. This was certainly the case in the former Soviet Union. In theocratic nations, a religious organization controls every area of society. This has been the case in parts of the Middle East, and the Roman Catholic Church so governed some parts of medieval Europe.

In the United States, the basic unit of society is the person; all institutions are subject to the individual. It is not entirely uncommon for children to emancipate themselves from their parents, and it is less uncommon for parishioners to withdraw their membership from churches. The federal government exists by the consent of governed individuals. Everything is based upon a social contract, and radical individualism accepts no authority except by tentative consent with loopholes and exit contingencies.

The biblical view of society does not focus primarily on individuals or on any single institution. It centers on a sphere of sovereignty within which many different institutions operate legitimately in God's order and design. Ideally these institutions come together to form community life. Because these institutions have their origin in God, none of them should act arbitrarily. Civil government is accountable to its citizens and ultimately to God. As such, it is the government's role to legislate morality. To some, this is an outrage. To others, it is a no-brainer. Space does not permit a full discussion of this idea, but we can gain a simple enough understanding to explain it to our kids. (Or maybe we could have them explain it to us.)

God has imprinted what is known as natural law on the human heart. This is a general understanding that certain things are just wrong and should not be done. We'll talk more about this in later chapters, but certain things are considered taboo in every culture. As depraved as our society has become (and it is no more depraved than some previous societies—check out a history book), God's natural law still exerts a restraining influence in our world. Because this is so, it is possible to have a wise government official who isn't a Christian. Again, to some, this is an outrage, and to others . . . well, Martin Luther said he'd prefer a wise Turk to a foolish Christian. Our top choice would be a wise Christian, but such people don't always run for office. When it comes to good governance, we can cooperate with non-Christians—not as allies, but as what Francis Schaeffer called *cobelligerents,* or people who band together to fight a common evil.

God calls us to bring corrupt structures more in line with his will. Much of what is written in the Bible is also written in nature, so we can seek to persuade the state to act justly without cramming religion down anyone's throat. Abortion laws, for example, need not be revoked because the Bible says so. Rather, society has agreed that killing innocent persons is wrong and that the government should protect the innocent. It is necessary to prove that a fetus is a person, and medical science points increasingly to that conclusion. We can now exert pressure on the government to protect the unborn for legal and scientific reasons, not just religious reasons.

We cannot legislate God's kingdom into existence, and that is not the government's job. But we can advance God's vision for this world through wise and righteous government structures.

These three divinely ordained institutions—the home, the church, and the government—are gifts from God. God has structured our world in this way to bring about the fullness of his plan. Each of these institutions is under attack by evil forces that seek to thwart God's plans. These three realms of authority hold the greatest potential for furthering God's kingdom, and they can do the greatest damage if they become corrupt. Therefore, it is vitally important that we do everything possible to strengthen them. Most importantly, we can pray for families, churches, and governments, and especially for the parents, pastors, and government officials who lead them.

Another thing we can do is *stop talking negatively about these leaders in front of our children.* We are not suggesting that you should never criticize or express an opinion, but consider what it does to your children if all they know is your dislike for certain parents, pastors, or presidents. If Christians spent as much time praying for their president or prime minister as they spent openly criticizing him, perhaps government structures would be quicker to align themselves with godly principles and biblically informed views.

WHEN WILL GOD MAKE EVERYTHING RIGHT?

John the Baptist sent men to find out whether or not Jesus was "the one who was to come," the one they were expecting (Matthew 11:2-5). Jesus reminded them of a quotation from Isaiah 61, saying, "Go back and report to John what you hear and see: The blind receive sight, the lame walk, those who have leprosy are cured, the deaf hear, the dead are raised, and the good news is preached to the poor." The purpose of Jesus' mission was to create a society in which injustices were undone and all persons were welcomed at the table where Jesus was the host. Jesus had already begun to usher in the Kingdom of God as Isaiah envisioned it.

Jesus told the religious rulers of his day, "If I drive out demons by the Spirit of God, then the kingdom of God has come upon you" (Matthew 12:28). By his life, Jesus ushered in a long-awaited kingdom that did not end when he died. It continues concretely today in those three divine institutions of the home, the church, and the government.

The kingdom Jesus began with his life, ministry, and death will not be complete until he returns. God's Kingdom has not yet come in its fullness, so we still live in a world fraught with pain, suffering, malevolence, and confusion. Believers speak of living between the beginning and the end. We live in the "already, but not yet" of the Kingdom of God. By this we mean that Jesus has already ushered in the Kingdom, but the final consummation of God's rule over every aspect of creation has yet to happen. On the time line of history, one day a little dot will read, "The End." The present order will cease, and Christ will take us all home.

When that happens, our existence will be perfect. Our kids won't leave their wet towels on their beds. Collectors won't call saying, "We didn't receive your payment on time and are assessing a late fee to your account." We won't feel grief over the loss of a beloved grandparent, and the nagging pain in our back will be gone. When the Kingdom is fully realized, we will know God, and God will be fully with us. But not yet . . .

Until Jesus' glorious appearing, we must live with two days on our calendars: *that* day and *this* day. The "between time"—*this* day—is vitally important. It is here where the ministry of Jesus Christ becomes excitingly real in the lives of his people.

WHY DOES ANY OF THIS MATTER?

When you ask "why" questions, you are delving deep into the realm of motive. Why does a friend donate blood once a month without fail? Most people hate to be stuck with needles, so there must be a good reason. Why does a lawyer making six figures a year leave her firm and work for the state just to represent poverty-stricken families in abuse cases? There has to be a good "why" behind her actions.

In Genesis 1, God gives us a pretty big hint as to why all this matters:

> God said, "Let us make man in our image, in our likeness, and let them rule over the fish of the sea and the birds of the air, over the livestock, over all the earth, and over all the creatures that move along the ground." So God created man in his own image,

in the image of God he created him; male and female he created them. God blessed them and said to them, "Be fruitful and increase in number; fill the earth." (Genesis 1:26-28)

To "be fruitful and increase" (some texts say "be fruitful and multiply") is a creative act. In the beginning, God created man *imago Dei* ("in the image of God"). This means that we can participate with God as cocreators. It is also a promise.

Christians experience God as a promise maker and a promise keeper. In biblical theology, God's promise-making is called "covenant." God is complete in himself and was under no compulsion to make the world. God does not create because he has to but because he wants to. God speaks creation into being (an amazing act in itself) and binds himself to it. When God brings something into being, he does not abandon it but provides for it. All of creation is dependent on God for its continued existence (just ask Noah!). God made a covenant—a promise—with creation, and he keeps his promises. God also makes promises to men and women, and throughout the biblical record, God has been faithful.

Because humans are created *imago Dei,* we can also be promise makers and promise keepers. We reflect God's holy image when we make and keep covenant with others. In this area, humanity is radically different from beasts and birds. By making and keeping promises, we fully participate in the lives of others. Keeping our word to our spouses, our children, and our coworkers allows us to contribute to relationships in a faithful and blessed way. Let's take a closer look at what we'll call the "FX Mandate," that is, God's command to men and women to "be fruitful [F] and multiply [X]."

The words of Genesis 1:28 can be narrowly construed as a command from God that needs to be obeyed. According to that interpretation, we procreate because God said we had to. This is not the only way to understand the verse, however. It is more fruitful to understand the mandate as a pronouncement of blessing. God tells those he loves to be fruitful and multiply so that they can share in the joyous blessing of giving themselves away. Being fruitful and multiplying bind you to something larger than yourself. This is one very important way for humans to participate in God's kingdom at this time.

Our mandate is to go forth and be a blessing, and—as the Hippocratic oath says—to "do no harm." We are responsible for not screwing things up. That is why God immediately follows the "be fruitful and multiply" pronouncement with instructions for living on this earth.

BEYOND THE W'S

It is no accident that the first and last words of Christ in the Gospel of John are questions. John intentionally structures his Gospel by using questions to help his readers better understand Jesus. Declarative statements immediately convey information, but questions help us to engage a subject. Questions are multidimensional. How many answers are there to the question, "Who are you?" Questions provide a starting point and a framework for simple or complex views. They can be road maps that provide a way into a topic and, often, a way out. Good questions are the building blocks of ideas. Besides helping us get into a subject, questions can bring out the best in us.

We ask, "Can a man fly?" And Orville and Wilbur glide over the dunes at Kitty Hawk as modern transportation is changed forever.

"How do we keep mothers who have recently delivered babies from dying in hospitals?" About 150 years ago, Dr. Ignaz Semmelweis in Vienna made his medical students wash their hands, and the mortality rate for new mothers dropped fivefold, resulting in the new medical field of infection control.

We ponder, "What does it mean to be a godly parent?" and perhaps we read a book on the subject.

"Why, Daddy?" is often a kid's favorite question.

"You need to brush your teeth and get your pajamas on," you tell your four-year-old.

"But why, Daddy?"

"Sweetie, don't hit your sister in the head with *Hop on Pop,*" you say to your two-year-old.

"Daddy, why not?"

"You can't multiply zero by anything and get a number other than zero," you explain to your eight-year-old.

"But Dad, why?"

"Daddy, where does the sun go at night?"

"Daddy, how come I have green eyes like Mommy, and Sis has brown eyes like Grandma, but no one has blue eyes like you?"

And you want to say, "Because Daddy is an alien!"

Children learn by asking questions. Did the grand questioner Socrates implicitly know that, or did he just luck out? Probably he knew. In many courses, especially in the upper levels of education, instructors teach students using the Socratic method, named for the ancient Greek philosopher who asked so many questions. Socrates liked to pass the time just talking. When a seemingly wise man would make a bold declaration regarding love, virtue, or justice, the philosopher would respond by asking a simple question.

"Can virtue be taught?" Meno asked Socrates.

"Can you tell me what virtue is?" Socrates responded.

Meno replied with a list of answers, and Socrates noted that Meno had made something that was one into something that was many. Socrates then asked Meno if there was a single, unified definition of virtue. Thus began a friendly dialogue discussing the essence of virtue in humanity and the nature of knowledge and learning. Although the discussion gets deep, it all began with a simple question.

We have used these wonderful *w* questions to summarize the irreducible answers to fundamental questions about meaning, purpose, and destiny. In so doing, we have picked up some useful—and profound—information.

It is important for you to know that you and your children are God's treasured possessions *(who)*. God's ultimate desire for humanity is to get all his kids home *(what)*. God's purposes are achieved in the arenas of home, church, and government *(where)*. God's kingdom rule is under way, and his Kingdom continues to work itself out in our lives; then one day time will come to an end and God will be all in all *(when)*. Lastly, we have the great fundamental question of *why?* God has empowered us to participate with him in the unspeakable blessing of advancing his work on this earth and in living out our true identities and destinies in the world to come.

part 3
What We Value

This section deals with three transcendental verities: truth, goodness, and beauty. Writers down through the ages, including such diverse characters as Plato, Augustine, Jonathan Edwards, and Hans Christian Andersen, have had something to say about these virtues. Plato wondered whether a thing was true because God declared it to be true, or if God declared it to be true because it was true. Christians believe that truth, goodness, and beauty are found in the person of God. Things are true, good, and beautiful because they correspond to God's character and nature. As parents, we can use things that are true, good, and beautiful to point our children to God, who created everything that exists.

Your little boy asks you to fix his toy truck. You say you'll do it later and go back to your own business. He recognizes that you're not giving his truck your full attention, so he asks, "Do you promise?" Now you're up against a wall. Your child is asking you for reassurance and commitment. If you promise and don't follow through, you will lose credibility. Suddenly fixing this toy has become very serious business. A child cannot imagine your violating a promise.

Your child is not asking anything of you that he wouldn't ask of himself. He asks if he can go in the backyard and play. You ask if he remembered to make his bed. "I'll do it later, Mom. *I promise!*" That's the beauty of a kid. He's ready to promise; the words flow easily out of his mouth. The thought that he might not follow through probably doesn't even cross his mind. If you doubt him, you get, "Really, Mom. I promise. Cross my heart and hope to die." And if he's *really* serious: "Cross my heart, hope to die, *stick a needle in my eye!*" It's a good thing we grow out of that kind of behavior!

Or do we?

When adults are about to testify in court, they traditionally place one hand on a Bible, raise the other hand and say, "I swear to tell the truth, the whole truth, and nothing but the truth, so help me God." For most people, there's not a lot of difference between that and "Cross my heart, hope to die, stick a needle in my eye."

Anyone who has ever purchased a house knows the great lengths to which we go to get someone to believe us. We sign our names countless times and pay an attorney to make sure that each *i* gets dotted and each *t* gets crossed.

Why is it necessary for people to swear with oaths and sign their names on the dotted line? The answer is simple: *People lie.*

We've all done it. How many of us can say we've never manufactured an excuse for being late or cheated on a test or denied saying something we actually said or told the kids it was past 8:00 P.M. when it wasn't? People are deceptive. We twist words, omit things, and manipulate meanings. We fudge a little here and a little there. We spin, shade, and distort things. We play little games so that we can say to ourselves, "Well, technically, I wasn't *really* lying."

Deception begins early for most of us, and we get better at it with practice. But in order for a community to survive, truth-telling is essential. It would be impossible to live in a world in which the truth was never told. When we ask a simple question such as, "Hey, is this hot?" we expect the truth, because the consequences could be serious.

We want people to tell us the truth. Usually we want to tell them the truth too, but we still like to reserve the option, on occasion, to deceive. The most famous example of this is when a wife asks, "Honey, does this outfit make me look fat?" and her husband quickly starts looking for loopholes.

DEFINING A LIE

Two small children are tugging at their mother, who is in the kitchen fixing supper. She hears the sound of an engine in the driveway and announces, "Daddy's home!" The children go charging out the front door and greet . . . the UPS guy. Assuming that her husband does not drive a UPS truck, did she tell a lie?

A father reads his three-year-old daughter a book about animals. He says to her, "Now, the frog says, 'Moo,' right?" She giggles and says, "No, Daddy, the frog says, 'Ribbit'!" He says, "Oh, that's right. I'm always getting those mixed up." Is he lying to her? Or is he just playing a harmless game?

The phone rings. A teenager picks it up and after a brief exchange says, "Mom, it's your boss."

Mom says, "Tell her I'm not home."

The teenager asks, "Isn't that lying?"

So Mom steps outside onto the back porch. "Okay, now tell her I'm not in."

Have we crossed the line yet? Do we even need to talk about telemarketers?

If telling the truth is serious business, then we had better get serious about recognizing the difference between truth and deception. What constitutes a lie? How about this simple definition: A lie is a statement (written, verbal, or communicated by body language) made with the intent to mislead someone. In the first scenario above, the mother didn't intend to mislead her children. She wasn't lying; she was mistaken. In the second situation, the father wasn't misleading his daughter; he was playing. In the third example, the mother was clearly trying to mislead her boss, and worse, she was using her teenager as an accomplice.

There are many debates about the proper philosophical understanding of truth, but everyone agrees that it is better to live in a society based on truth-telling than in one based on lies. The concept of truth may vary slightly according to when and where you live, but truth-telling is a universally desirable quality.

For some reason, however, many of us "manage" the truth instead of living it. According to virtually any report or poll on the subject, we've become a pragmatic people, a people of the lie, a Pinocchio nation.

For most of us, the word *Pinocchio* conjures up images of lying. Carlo Collodi's imaginative story tells of a wooden puppet that comes to life and learns a lesson about the danger of telling lies. In the famous scene where his nose grows to ridiculous lengths, Pinocchio is asked a question about some gold coins by the Fairy with blue hair:

> "And the four pieces—where have you put them?" asked the Fairy.

"I have lost them!" said Pinocchio, but he was telling a lie, for he had them in his pocket.

He had scarcely told the lie when his nose, which was already long, grew at once two inches longer.

"And where did you lose them?"

"In the wood near here."

At this second lie his nose went on growing.

"If you have lost them in the wood near here," said the Fairy, "we will look for them and we shall find them: because everything that is lost in that wood is always found."

"Ah! now I remember all about it," replied the puppet, getting quite confused; "I didn't lose the four gold pieces, I swallowed them whilst I was drinking your medicine."

At this lie his nose grew to such an extraordinary length that poor Pinocchio could not move in any direction. If he turned to one side he struck his nose against the bed or the window-panes, if he turned to the other he struck it against the walls or the door, if he raised his head a little he ran the risk of sticking it into one of the Fairy's eyes.

And the Fairy looked at him and laughed.

"What are you laughing at?" asked the puppet, very confused and anxious at finding his nose growing so prodigiously.

"I am laughing at the lie you have told."

"And how can you possibly know that I have told a lie?"

"Lies, my dear boy, are found out immediately, because they are of two sorts. There are lies that have short legs, and lies that have long noses. Your lie, as it happens, is one of those that have a long nose."

Pinocchio, not knowing where to hide himself for shame, tried to run out of the room; but he did not succeed, for his nose had increased so much that it could no longer pass through the door.[1]

WHAT IS TRUTH?

Wouldn't it be great if everyone grew longer noses or shorter legs upon telling a lie? Unfortunately, we have so mastered the art of managing the truth that there is often little or no physical evidence of our falsehoods. With straight faces and earnest tones, crooked politicians, shady salespeople, and (who are we kidding?) regular folks like us say whatever is necessary to get elected, close the deal, get ahead, or just avoid trouble. Telling and hearing the truth can no longer be considered a given in our society. How did we reach this point? And why, exactly, is telling the truth so difficult?

We've already defined a lie as a statement made with the intent to mislead someone. *Webster's New World Dictionary* says that truth is "the quality or state of being true, the quality of being in accordance with experience, facts, or reality; conformity with fact, agreement with a standard rule, etc., that accords with fact or reality."[2] The Greek word used for truth in the New Testament is *alatheia*. Its definition is a little more intuitive than *Webster's,* meaning something like "the stuff reality is made of."

So what exactly do we mean when we talk about telling the truth? Rubel Shelly has pointed out that there are two kinds of truth: factual truth and moral truth.[3] Telling the factual truth has to do with our understanding of reality. The mother who says, "Daddy's home!" when she hears the UPS truck is not telling the factual truth. Telling the moral truth is doing our best to line up what we say with the facts as we know them. It is this moral aspect of truth-telling that concerns us the most, although Christians should be factually correct as often as possible. God does not require Christians to be omniscient, but he does require them to be honest. We need not have the full content of factual truth, but we need to be trustworthy in using the facts at our disposal.

TRUTH OR CONSEQUENCES

People like to debate the content of truth and how we communicate our understanding of reality, but it is hard to live with any other definition of truth than the one we have given here. If our definition of truth is simply "that which is most advantageous for me," how are we going to answer questions such as "Is this hot?" or "Is that poisonous?"

As social beings, we have entered into a social contract with those around us. The premise behind evolutionary psychology is that humans are only capable of acting out of self-interest. According to naturalism, we are only concerned with the propagation of the species, and specifically with our own bloodline. This understanding of human nature denies our ability to be self-sacrificing or noble, suggesting as it does that we are simply body parts and nerve endings, and that our instinctual drives leave us no choice but to extend our gene pool into the future—often at the cost of someone else's gene pool.

According to this line of thought, why should we tell the truth to others? We would only do so if it would somehow be advantageous for us. The psalmist, in contrast, portrays a man who "keeps his oath even when it hurts" (Psalm 15:4).

What started out sounding like a call to freedom (we are free from narrow definitions of truth that have bound us in the past) ends up as a sentence of slavery (we are incapable of telling others the truth unless it seems beneficial to us). At first it sounds like an affirmation of human dignity (every individual has the ability to determine what is true for himself), but in the end it affirms our depravity (no one is able to just tell it like it is).

To this God says, "No, that is not true. You *are* capable of telling the truth. You can do this because you were made in my image, and I am truth. Yes, this image has been cracked by the Fall and your hearts are wicked and deceitful. But they do not have to be this way. You can be a truth-telling person—even when it hurts you. You don't have to tell the truth to get what you want. Being the kind of person who can tell the truth—simply and without fear—*is* what you want."

There are practical rewards for being an honest person. For example, truth breeds trust, and trust is the glue that holds human relationships together. Therefore, honest people have more rewarding and long-lasting relationships than dishonest people. In his book *The Different Drum,* M. Scott Peck suggests that God planted a desire in human hearts for open and honest relationships—what Peck calls communal relationships. When we distort the truth in order to keep the peace, we live in pseudo-communal relationships instead. These relationships aren't very satisfying, and they don't last. When we sow dishonesty, we reap alienation.

Ethicist Sissela Bok discusses the clear connection between honesty and trust:

> I can have different types of trust: that you will treat me fairly, that you will have my interests at heart, that you will do me no harm. But if I do not trust your word, can I have genuine trust in the first three? If there is no confidence in the truthfulness of others, is there any way to assess their fairness, their intentions to help or to harm? How, then, can they be trusted? Whatever matters to human beings, trust is the atmosphere in which it thrives.[4]

Telling the truth doesn't guarantee fantastic relationships, but it sure does improve the odds. Honesty allows us to live with dignity, integrity, and courage.

TO TELL THE TRUTH

Honesty is important for our world. It is the basis of order and the foundation of trust. Without honesty, we are more likely to experience broken relationships and dysfunction at all levels of society. Honesty is also important to God. He is Truth, so anything other than truth is the antithesis of God. A relationship with God begins and must continue in honesty because you can only meet God in the real world. You cannot meet the true God in a fantasyland. He lives in reality; or rather, reality lives in him.

But humans are prone to dishonesty. So far as we know, no one has ever had to teach a child to lie. It seems to come naturally. We do have to teach children (and ourselves) to be radical truth-tellers. It is one thing to value honesty—putting it into practice is something else entirely. Most people agree that lying is a bad thing and God does not like it. But it sure is a nice option to have tucked in your back pocket—just in case. We're like the child in Sunday school who gets two Bible verses mixed up and says, "A lie is an abomination unto the Lord and a very present help in time of need."

God's people should be truthful, and that won't happen until we make a commitment to speak the truth even when it hurts. That means that we should count the cost of truth-telling and be prepared to endure whatever discomfort might result. Most of us lie primarily to avoid pain. Making a commitment to truth means being willing to endure that pain. It is better not to make casual promises unless we know that we will be able to follow through. No more saying things just to make people think that we are nicer, friendlier, or more spiritual than we really are. No more looking for loopholes after we've gotten ourselves into a mess.

Perhaps the most practical way to maintain a firm commitment to honesty is to have fewer conversations. "When words are many, sin is not absent" (Proverbs 10:19). Another translation of this verse says sin is "unavoidable" (NASB). One way to raise the level of truthfulness in our conversations is to be "quick to listen, slow to speak" (James 1:19). In his sovereign wisdom, God gave us two ears but only one mouth. Perhaps we could demonstrate an important lesson to our children by listening twice as much as we speak.

TELLING THE TRUTH IN LOVE

This classic statement about telling the truth comes from the apostle Paul's letter to the church at Ephesus. He writes, "Speaking the truth in love, we will in all things grow up into him who is the Head, that is, Christ" (Ephesians 4:15). The phrase "speaking the truth" actually comes from a Greek word that means something like "truthing." The goal is to live the truth in what we think, do, and say. Truth must be our lifestyle when we follow the man who claimed to be the Truth.

One day a rich young ruler came to Jesus. His life was on the wrong track, so he asked Jesus, "What do I need to do?"

Jesus knew that he had to tell this guy a hard truth. He could have said, "Oh, you're fine. Just keep going the way you're going, and everything will work out eventually."

Jesus didn't do that. He said, "You should sell everything you own—give up life as you know it—and follow me." [5]

That seems a little harsh, doesn't it? This was a good kid—just a little mixed-up—and we want Jesus to be nice. But Jesus is more interested in telling the truth than being nice. Jesus wants his followers to be tactful, but he never wants us to gloss over the truth in such situations. A person's eternal destiny is more important than keeping the truth to ourselves.

Jesus said what he did because he loved the young man. Jesus loved people enough to tell them the truth. Truth and love must never be separated from each other. We all know people who love to speak the hard truth, and some believe that this is their spiritual gift. But Jesus never encourages us to damage others with our truth-telling.

Truth without love is a destructive weapon. Some people swing truth like a club and smash people's lives with it, but that kind of behavior grows out of selfishness and distrust. Truth is inherently powerful and can stand on its own. We are to speak the truth in love. We should never "vomit" the truth on people. If our motive is anything but love—if we need to prove a point or make people pay for the error of their ways—we should keep our mouths shut. Truth is always to be spoken in love.

RECEIVING THE TRUTH

We all want our children to tell us the truth. Some of us may prefer blissful ignorance, but for the most part we want our children to know that they can always come to us with the truth. We tell them, "You can come to me with anything." But are we really prepared to receive truth from our kids? That's something we ought to think about.

Children are a lot like adults. They deceive in order to avoid pain or discomfort. If we want our children to be honest with us, it is counterproductive to blow up when they finally do tell us the truth. We can best receive the truth with our mouths closed and our eyes and ears open. If we keep our emotions from becoming volatile, our children are more likely to share the truth openly. If our children are afraid of our emotional reactions to the truth, they are more often tempted to deceive us. We must be careful not to teach them by our actions that truth-telling has worse consequences than telling a lie.

Consider your own relationship with God. When we confess the truth to God, he doesn't explode and berate us. God helps us pick up the pieces and move forward in dealing with the natural consequences of our behavior.

We also want children who keep short accounts with God, children who are quick to confess. When our child musters the courage to tell us the truth about something he's done, we should respect that honesty. Taking things personally and saying, "How could you do this to me?" only clouds the issue and confuses the child. We should communicate to our children that everything is going to be okay and that there is always a solution, as long as we're honest. There are long-term benefits to taking this approach.

Remember your son's toy truck? What happens when it's *your* truck—the one parked in the garage? We hope that you've honed your truth-telling skills by the time he's seventeen and comes to ask you for the keys, or you may be tempted to say that you've lost them. Let's say that you tell him he *can* take the truck out for a spin. It's past midnight and he's still not home. No phone call, no text message. When he finally comes home and tells you that he backed your truck into his friend's mom's BMW, the foundation you've established during his childhood years of modeling and receiving truth will become all-important.

The fact that he told you about it at all is a pretty good sign.

Robert Philip Hanssen was a veteran FBI agent assigned to the counterintelligence program. He was also a spy for the Russians. During the fifteen years that he sold American secrets to Moscow, he was meticulously careful to cover his tracks. But he was not careful enough. On February 18, 2001, Hanssen was arrested for espionage.

Experts say that Hanssen was one of the most destructive spies in U.S. history in terms of compromised intelligence, financial cost, and loss of human life.[1] He revealed the identities of at least two Soviet agents who were sent back to Moscow and executed. In order to avoid the death penalty himself, Hanssen agreed to a plea that led to a life sentence without the possibility of parole.

What makes this story especially dark and difficult to understand is that Hanssen was a devout Christian, especially devoted to his wife, his family, and pro-life causes. He and his wife marched in anti-abortion rallies and displayed pro-life bumper stickers on the family van that transported their six children to and from church and private school. When coworkers held parties at strip clubs, he refused to attend, saying that it would be a sin. He routinely told friends that without religion, people were lost.[2] He took a friend with him to church the day he was arrested.

Those closest to Hanssen were devastated when his double life was revealed. When asked how a man of such strong moral convictions could have engaged in such unethical behavior, they could only guess that he "must have been able to compartmentalize his life, deluding himself into thinking that espionage was simply an exciting intellectual challenge that had nothing to do with leading a good, moral Christian life." [3] He wasn't able to compartmentalize as well as people thought, however. Things started to spill over as other areas of his life were compromised.

Obviously, what Robert Hanssen did was wrong on many levels. There were both measurable and incalculable consequences. How do you compute the effect of giving away America's plan to keep its government running and its leaders safe in the aftermath of a nuclear attack?

No one disputes that what Hanssen did was bad. But what made it bad? That's what we can't seem to articulate. He betrayed his country, lied to his wife, and sold information that cost other people their lives. He separated his life into segments and kept at least one of those segments hidden from everyone for years. All of these things are wrong, but saying that doesn't get us any closer to answering the question, *Why* was Robert Hanssen's behavior bad? How do we know? Is there some standard we can apply in making such a judgment?

In old Westerns, it was much easier; good guys wore white hats and bad guys wore black hats. In reality, though, no one is completely good, and we can't say for certain that anyone is totally bad. Maybe we should all go out and buy gray hats.

Civilized societies throughout history have agreed that there is a difference between good and evil. Many of those societies seem to have had much less trouble with the question than we do. This is un- derstandable because their worlds were more homogenous than ours. Public opinion dominates our pluralistic culture, and advertisers take the attitude that a majority opinion determines what we will receive in life. But thinking people still have the right to choose between good and evil, regardless of what they are offered. For Christians, this is a responsibility.

It seems difficult for us to find standards for good and evil in twenty-first-century America, but it is not beyond us. Somewhere deep in our hearts, we just *know*. Still, just knowing is not enough.

GOOD, BAD, AND HOW TO MEASURE

There's a consensus that some behaviors are good and some behaviors are bad. My neighbor found out that my edger was broken and came over to do the edging for me. He's a good guy, no doubt. Someone rudely cuts me off in traffic, and that seems bad. Helping victims of a hurricane is good. Child abuse is bad. Providing Christmas gifts and goodies for families who don't have the money to make it through the holidays is good. Torture and rape are universally condemned. Yet few of us stop to ask why this is so. Is there a valid reason to categorize some behaviors as good and others as bad? How do we teach our children to determine the difference for themselves when we're not around to help them?

Several years ago at a conference of the American Academy of Religion and the Society of Biblical Literature, in a session titled "Biblical Authority and Homosexuality," one pro-homosexual panelist told the audience, "Scripture contains no timeless, normative moral truths."

A member of the audience stood up and responded, "I'm rather confused. I'm a pastor, and people constantly ask me if something they have done is wrong and if they need forgiveness. For example, isn't it always wrong to abuse a child?"

A female panelist issued this shocking response: "What counts as abuse differs from society to society; so we can't really use the word *abuse* without tying it to a historical context." [4]

Wow! It's hard to imagine that anyone could really believe that. Are the categories of "good" and "bad" that nebulous? Are they just social constructs that can vary so widely from culture to culture that they might be considered irrelevant in our *multicultural* environment? Is there any common basis from which we can determine how to live?

Without an external source of truth, trying to tell good from bad can be confusing and dangerous. The apostle Paul talks about people who "measure themselves by themselves and compare themselves with themselves," adding that "they are not wise" (2 Corinthians 10:12). Without a perfect standard, we have no measure for making judgments of any kind.

As parents who must train our kids to discern right from wrong, we must find that perfect standard.

MARGARET MEAD AND AN ABDICATION OF JUDGMENT

The late anthropologist Margaret Mead (1901–1978) is considered the patron saint of cultural relativism. Using her research among people in Samoa, Mead refuted the universality of ethical standards, particularly in terms of sex and sexuality. She argued that standards of right and wrong or good and bad differ widely from culture to culture. Therefore, she determined, we have no basis for saying that one set of behaviors is superior to another. We can only say what is generally considered acceptable for one generation in one culture. Her book *Coming of Age in Samoa*, first published in 1928, is regarded by many as a precursor to the sexual revolution in the United States.[5]

Mead's tolerance masquerades as higher thinking. It claims to be responsible and humane by offering a higher level of respect, sympathy, and support for whatever a group of human beings chooses to believe. However, abdicating moral judgment about behavior isn't kind, wise, or responsible. When we turn people into puppets of their surrounding culture rather than affirming them as individuals created in the image of God, we rob them of their dignity as responsible moral agents.

"The elimination of judgment, the evacuation of the very capacity of judging, would spell the end of the human subject as a self-respecting, accountable being. Judging is a sign, a mark, of our respect for the dignity of others and ourselves," writes Jean Bethke Elshtain, social and political ethics professor at the University of Chicago Divinity School. [6]

In other words, when we tell a person that what he has done is bad, we honor him by separating who he is from what he has done: "You know better than that. You are capable of good." Unlike animals, humans have the ability and the freedom to say no to their desires. This is a good thing when it helps us to avoid something bad. As Augustine said, "The soul lives by avoiding what it dies by desiring." [7]

We *do* know better. The Bible says that God's law has been written on our hearts and that it operates in our consciences.[8] As much as we may wish to avoid it, something inside tells us when we are not behaving as we should.

Several Web sites allow people to post confessions of their sins anonymously. This clearly demonstrates that much of the time people *know* when they're doing something wrong. One of these sites even indexes confessions into categories based on the seven deadly sins. Reading many of these confessions, you can feel the grief and remorse coming through the words posted:

> You know, you read statistics but feel that it will never happen to you. It did. I got pregnant. I got pregnant with a man who just stopped loving me one day. I got pregnant and had an abortion. I'm not even old enough to buy alcohol, but I watched as they sucked out my first child. . . . You have no idea, none of you. It will never stop hurting, ever. I'm completely alone. . . . No one loves me. I am completely unlovable. Do you know how that feels? Does anyone?

> I am only 14, but I have a relationship with a much older guy. My parents would be really mad if they found out. I guess it's only been a couple of weeks, but I feel like I'm in love. The thing is, I don't even know his real name. He goes by "The Lion."

> Why didn't I settle for the less expensive TV? I wanted to impress my neighbor—but now I don't have enough money to make the payment on it. The store called again today, wondering if I was going to make it in by the weekend to pay them. I always do this—and at 50 years old, you'd think I would have learned some lessons by now.

> I envy my flatmate that she can stay single and not feel like she is rejected. I envy that she actually doesn't need a man to complete her life. I envy that she is thinner than me. I envy that she is stronger than me. I envy that she is a better friend than me. I envy her cooking. I envy her hair . . . oh, dear . . . I pretty much envy everything about her.

I don't go out, I don't want to work, I can't be bothered to start up any friendships. Maybe it's depression, I don't know. It's been this way since I was little, but now that I have a son it bothers me; I don't want him to have a pathetic dad.

I'm so fed up with lying. I lie to everyone. It's getting worse. I can't remember who I've told what to. I want to just be honest. Now that I'm thinking about it, I'm not sure why I don't just tell the truth. I don't know why I felt like I had to lie. It's too late to come clean now. I've told too much to too many people. I wish I hadn't. I wish I could take it all back.

I will destroy others to get ahead in this world. I am two-faced, and I am not proud of it. [9]

Something tells us that there is a profound difference between how we sometimes behave and how we *ought* to behave. As Greg Koukl puts it, moral norms "have a force we can actually feel *prior* to any behavior. This is called the incumbency, the 'oughtness' of morality. . . . It appeals to our will, compelling us to act in a certain way, though we may disregard its force and choose not to obey." [10]

When a person chooses not to follow that moral directive, she usually feels guilt and shame, as is clearly witnessed to by the above confessions. People who succeed in completely overcoming their consciences are called "sociopaths" because they are a danger to society. They aren't dangerous because they subvert the social norms; they are dangerous because they injure other people.

It's not wise to ignore our consciences. Bad ideas and bad behavior have bad consequences. They have the potential to shatter the peace of God (shalom), the wholeness, health, and rightness that God wants his people to experience and exhibit.

THE COMPOSER'S ORIGINAL INTENT

C. S. Lewis, like many others, has argued compellingly that there are values that transcend a particular culture. [11] But what is it about a value or a behavior that makes it good or bad? What is our source for determining the *value* of a particular value? Is it simply that which is best for the propagation of our species? That's the position of the evolutionary biologists and psychologists of the world. Helping the weak, the handicapped, and the needy does nothing to advance the survival of the fittest. Protecting a child from abuse works *against* such survival. So why do we feel a sense of duty to help those less fortunate than ourselves? We're not talking about a *desire* to help someone, but about a feeling that we *ought* to help someone. Those are two very different things. Lewis expresses it this way: "Suppose you hear a cry for help from a man in danger. You will probably feel two desires—one a desire to give help . . . , the other a desire to keep out of danger. . . . But you will find inside you, in addition to these two impulses to help, a third thing which tells you that you ought to follow the impulse to help, and suppress the impulse to run away."[12]

Lewis explains the problem we encounter when we have two conflicting instincts. Naturally, the stronger instinct should win, but something in our hearts tells us to choose the weaker of the two instincts. Lewis calls this "Moral Law."

Using the illustration of a piano, Lewis says that there are no "good notes" and "bad notes." Each note may be good at one time and bad at another. What determines the goodness or badness of the note is something other than the note itself or any other note. It is something higher, something transcendent: the sheet music that says what tune to play. In other words, what makes an impulse or an action good or bad is whether or not it correlates with the composer's original intent.

Now we're really getting to something: the Composer's original intent. We are the masterpieces of our Creator,[13] the great Composer who *himself* is the standard against which all of our actions must be measured. It's not about randomly pulling a bunch of laws out of our Bibles and attempting to abide by them. It's about godliness. Jesus is the most perfect picture we have of God, so he is the One against whom we must measure all things. Christlikeness and Christ-closeness continuously transform a person who reflects his image. This transformation is real worship, and only when we are transformed are we able to judge.[14] To determine good or evil, we ask, "Is this Christlike? Will this bring me closer to God?" This raises the bar, but it also makes the standard much clearer. It honors us by recognizing that we are moral beings who are able to make choices. This sort of judging is appropriate for beings who have been created with free will.

GOOD GIRL, GOOD BOY—WHAT'S THE MATTER WITH US?

What are we saying to our children when we say that we want them to be "good little boys and girls"? It might be best to avoid such talk altogether. Telling a child to be a "good boy" or not to be a "bad girl" gives them nothing to *do*—that is, no instruction to follow—and it may lead them to believe that they are either good or bad persons. Although we do bad things because we are bad people (sinners), this is not the *whole* truth about us, and we need to be sure that it is not the only truth we are communicating to our kids. Speaking to our children in such absolute terms can lead them into an oppressive, shame-filled life.

Clearly there is something wrong with us. We sometimes do bad things without thinking about it, and we often have to force ourselves to do good things. What is bad seems to come naturally; what is good requires effort and intentionality. Until we get a handle on what makes a thing good or bad, we will not know how to fix it.

An action isn't good because God arbitrarily decided that he liked one thing but not another. An action is good because it exemplifies his nature. Conversely, a behavior is not bad because of some capricious decision of God, but because that behavior is inconsistent with his goodness.

God is Ultimate Reality, so whether we are talking about what is true, what is good, or what is beautiful, we are really talking about reflecting some aspect of God. For example, God cannot lie or say that lying is good because truth is fundamental to his nature.[15] Telling the truth corresponds to God's character and is therefore a good thing to do. Lying is bad because it is ungodly (that is, unlike God).

Greed isn't evil just because we have agreed upon generosity as a desirable social norm. Greed is the opposite of God's generous nature, so it will always be bad, regardless of what a culture decides. All of the qualities we want our kids to develop as they grow up—kindness, patience, endurance, forgiveness—are attributes of God. As people made in God's image, we are designed to become more like him as we grow up.

God is fundamentally good, so being good is godly. God is not bad, so being bad is ungodly. In order to even have a conversation about good and bad, there has to be a standard. Otherwise, when what seems good for me is bad for you, we are on a path to anarchy and chaos.

The topic of evil is so difficult to discuss because by using the term *evil*, we are suggesting that there is some standard that tells us what is and is not evil in a given circumstance. But who gets to say what that standard is? Is anyone willing to step forward and suggest they are qualified to make such an assessment? We cannot measure ourselves by ourselves; it just doesn't work. Can we allow social consensus to decide for us?

At one time in our nation, the consensus was that slavery was acceptable, even good. Women and children, too, were treated like property. The only people who had rights were white adult men who owned land. Lynching was acceptable, but interracial marriages were not. Bearing this in mind, does anyone *really* want to advocate that society be allowed to determine right and wrong for individuals? The Roman concept of *vox populae, vox dei* ("the voice of the people is the voice of god") has dangerous consequences.

PARENTING TOWARD GODLINESS

Here's what this means for parents: When you say that you want your kids to "be good," you're really saying that you want them to be like God. What you thought was a propositional truth (goodness) turns out to be a person (God). This is very important because it could mean that some parenting manuals and techniques are built on faulty foundations. Rather than teaching our kids to know right from wrong and good from bad, we should be teaching our kids to know and imitate God.

The best way to do that is to introduce them to Jesus, who is God made flesh. The whole premise behind "WWJD" (a concept that has been too much maligned) is that we can and ought to live as Jesus would live if he were in our shoes. This guides our parenting much better than asking our kids to follow a lot of frustrating rules that even we can't keep track of. It may be more difficult to decide what Jesus would do in a given situation, but it's better to have our children wrestle with that than to have them obey without knowing the why behind the what.

In this book, we've talked about Jesus as the model for our parenting. What if Jesus was the model for our kids as well? Why not redefine successful parenting in such a way that the goal is for our kids to become like Jesus? That's good!

The goal can't simply be better behavior. Jesus became most angry with fairly well-behaved people. Unfortunately, many parenting books provide us with a recipe for good behavior that isn't tied to good motives. According to God, this is inferior to bad behavior with good motives. Could many of our parenting approaches actually be helping us to raise Pharisees instead of disciples of Jesus? It's a terrible thing to contemplate, but until we deal with the fundamental flaws in our parenting strategies, we won't be able to offer any meaningful alternatives.

Because kids who grow up to be good grow up to be like Jesus, it's important to know how Jesus grew up. In Luke 2:52 we read, "Jesus grew in wisdom and stature, and in favor with God and men." We may be stuck with our stature—we can't worry or pray ourselves into being any taller or shorter—but we can do something about the three other growth areas that Luke mentions: growth in wisdom, in favor with God, and in favor with people.

Simply put, our parenting should help our kids determine what is wise, what pleases God, and what helps them get along with people. As we study our Bibles to find the answers to these questions, it will help if we shift our focus from "What does this passage tell me to do?" to "What does this passage say about God?" The more we teach our children about God's nature and Jesus' character, the more we will be able to help them to make wise choices, gain God's favor, and get along with their siblings or playmates.

Perhaps you are frustrated because we haven't given you specific instructions, but specifics are up to you. We aren't offering tips about how to get your kids home by curfew or how to make them get straight As in school. That's your job. What we do ask is that you instill a love for Scripture in your kids, a love based on the love they have for the One who inspired it.

THE ONE TRUE STANDARD

At the beginning of the chapter, we left a question unanswered pending our discussion of good vs. bad. We now return to that question—*Why* was Robert Hanssen's behavior bad?—better equipped to answer it. What Robert Hanssen did was bad because it contradicted the fact that he was created in the image of a perfect, loving, and true God, whose desire is that all people come to know him and be like his Son, Jesus. Hanssen's betrayal of his faith, his family, and his country runs counter to everything Christlike.

Jesus is the standard against whom all things must be measured. What is like him and leads us closer to him is good. What is unlike him and moves us away from him is bad. Everything else is just details.

Chapter 9
Beautiful vs. Ugly

Beauty seems to be a matter of opinion and preference rather than a matter of objective standards. It is difficult to claim, "This is beauty," without sounding ethnocentric and unnecessarily dogmatic. Is there really such a thing as an objectively beautiful poem or work of art or—well, anything? Is it all just a matter of taste? Does how, when, and where we are raised determine what we think is beautiful? Or is there something about which all people everywhere can agree, "This is beauty"?

And why does any of this matter?

IN THE EYE OF THE BEHOLDER?

Of all the things that parents can teach their children, there is perhaps nothing as distinctive as offering them an objective standard of beauty. When a child spends time in another household, something as trivial as the "correct" way to make macaroni and cheese comes under close scrutiny. This merely illustrates the difficulty of talking generically about differences without filtering them through our own personal worldviews.

Perhaps a large part of the friction between what we find to be positively stunning and what seems utterly revolting comes from our limited view of culture. For instance, though there are places in the world where a tattooed body is deemed a work of art, there are quite a number of other cultures that disagree. On the flip side, we've seen in recent years that even when women in Afghanistan are not required to wear a traditional veil, they do so anyway to preserve their modesty.[1] Meanwhile, Western cultural standards of dress have continued to grow looser in terms of what kind of exposure is acceptable. It seems that the old maxim is true: Beauty is in the eye of the beholder.

Or is it? The problem with trying to find an impartial standard of beauty is in the criteria we use. It's happened before: Two people are looking at the same piece of art. One person is moved to tears; the other is moved to leave the room. In such situations, the popular notion is to agree to disagree, but is that the standard God wants us to impart to our children? Is there a good metaphor that will help a child understand the intangible beauty of the Lord?

Regardless of our theological position, it's hard to argue against there being an intentional order and rhythm in creation. Look at the cycle of the four seasons or the food chain's "circle of life" (as a certain animated lion explained to his son). In spite of obvious cultural differences, the vast majority of people have always considered nature to be beautiful and have regarded destruction as ugly.

Ironically, the so-called primitive cultures recognize these universals more quickly than societies based on consumerism. Perhaps this has something to do with the pace at which they live. Psalm 46:10 tells us to "be still, and know that I am God." Beauty transfixes us, quieting the commotion of our daily lives and making us still. Most people affirm that the best response to a rainbow, a field of wildflowers, or a frozen waterfall is silence.

In this way beauty helps us to know that God is God, and God is good.

Even the atheist philosopher Anthony O'Hear contends that by experiencing beauty, we feel ourselves to be in contact with a deeper reality than the everyday.[2] To experience beauty, we must calm ourselves and slow down. The experience of beauty can be described in a variety of ways, but none of them includes the word *hurry*.

THE DEEP END

In parenting, this undeniable deeper reality gives us a place to begin in teaching our children about the beauty of the Creator. Whether we are looking at the brilliant colors of a sunset or making a special vacation trek to a waterfall with glittering rock formations, the simple truth is that our understanding of God's beauty is often tied to our perception of his handiwork. One author asks, "Why does beauty take our breath away? Why does it pull at our eyes and heart? The answer at first seems obvious: we like beautiful things. But there is a deeper reality. A quest for beauty lies within the heart of every person. We search it out, whether we actively realize it or not, and recognizing the cause of our search is actually a key to understanding our deepest longings and our true humanity."[3]

Imagine a little girl walking at the edge of a great ocean on a windy day. As the tide rolls in, she begins to conform her footsteps to the water's rhythm, running in toward the shore as the ripples reach the beach, then chasing the waves a few steps back again.

As this process continues, the girl wonders if it would be safe to step in further, and so she goes close enough to let her feet, then legs become submerged. She feels that she is becoming a part of the ocean while still maintaining her position on the beach. Soon she finds herself less in control and more in awe of the strength of the waves. Thankfully, one of her parents is nearby and snatches her out of trouble before she's fully engulfed. As parent and child make their way back up the beach, the girl wonders if going back in the water is a good idea. She has developed a sense that the world is bigger than what she can control, but with her parents close by, she is not alone in figuring that out. She has successfully (and safely) explored the beauty of the Creator while maintaining a respect for his power.

When we explore the beauty of the Creator with our children, we realize that it is not a one-sided journey. Pastor and author Brian McLaren told us this story about the lasting blessings of sharing a love of beauty with his kids:

> It was one of those long car rides with our four small kids in the back of the minivan. They all started snoozing at the same time, which gave Grace and me a chance for a good, deep talk. What were our goals beyond surviving toddlerhood? What

were our dreams beyond diapers and keeping a supply of crayons in the house?

Given the chance, dreams sometimes pop into our hearts without warning, and one did that day. I told Grace I'd like to take each of our kids on a trip, just that child and me, somewhere outside the United States, before they graduated from high school. It would be expensive, and we didn't have much discretionary income; but we felt it was a good, fun, and potentially formative idea, so we said yes.

Years passed, and we designed the trips to match my schedule and each child's personality. My eldest, Rachel, met up with me in France, and we toured Southern Europe together, taking in history, culture, and beautiful scenery, and meeting some wonderful missionaries. I'll never forget Rachel's face as we sat with a delightful French pastor and his wife in a restaurant near Avignon; she was exposed to a stellar cultural experience and to some exemplary Christians who treated her like an honored guest.

Brett's trip was very different—he joined me while I spoke at a conference in Costa Rica. But as soon as the event ended, we headed for the jungle on an amazing adventure, first with friends, and then just the two of us. When the first night fell in the rain forest, the sound of countless singing insects and frogs rose louder and louder. We looked at each other, wide-eyed. What an amazing world God has made!

Trevor joined me for a trip to the Galapagos Islands, which gave us a chance to indulge our shared love of biology in one of the most fascinating ecosystems in the world, and allowed us to interact with other people on our tour. So many conversations about God ensued, prompting Trevor to quip to his pastor-dad, "Wow, you never get a break, do you?" For the rest of my life, the words *joy* and *freedom* will always be associated with a memory of Trev and me swimming and swirling with sea lions in the blue Pacific.

Jodi, our youngest, joined me last year for a trip through Africa, where she saw natural beauty and human suffering poignantly juxtaposed every day. She also met wonderful Christians of many languages and tribes. For a young woman coming of age and seeking her own faith, not a hand-me-down from her parents, it was a formative time with lasting effects.

I don't know what my kids will remember about me when I'm gone, but I don't think it will be my sermons or books, my parental lectures, or even my faithful provision for their physical needs. I think it will be that I love God's world—the people in it, its oceans and forests, its amazing creatures and glorious vistas. On those trips, they saw me happily enjoying varied cultures and exciting adventures and keeping alive my thirst for learning. All of these flow from my identity as a follower of Jesus, a child of God, the One who made this amazing planet and all it contains. If that's all they inherit from me, it will be enough. [4]

I.O.U.—INWARD, OUTWARD, UPWARD

Beauty can slow our pace or stop us in our tracks. What happened when you saw that special someone and "just knew" that she was different? What did you feel the first time you laid eyes on your child? What happened inside of you the last time you stood outside on a cold night and looked up at a clear sky full of stars? Try to recall specifically how your body reacted. What was your physical response? If you think about it, you may discover that most of the time such moments cause a multilayered response involving an inward reflection, an outward reaction, and an upward gaze.

In those moments, the inward reflection hearkens back to innocence. The creation story didn't begin with Genesis 3 (the fall of man), but with the two chapters prior, in which humankind lived in an innocent rhythm with God, the rest of creation, and each other. "God said, 'Let us make man in our image, in our likeness, and let them rule over the fish of the sea and the birds of the air, over the livestock, over all the earth, and over all the creatures that move along the ground'" (Genesis 1:26).

Before you go off to confront a lion or tiger with this quote, please recognize that when humans chose a path away from God's plan, we surrendered the splendor of this ideal. In Isaiah 11:6-9, we find the promise that one day the Messiah will restore this plan, but we currently live in a broken world that knows nothing of its reality. An occasional glimpse of beauty allows us to peek through the dirty picture frame and uncover the true masterpiece hidden beneath.

It seems that children are able to see this much more quickly than adults. An innocent child might approach a stranger in a mall to say hello, while we panic into hyperprotective mode, fearing he'll be kidnapped. We do need to safeguard our children, but preventing them from exploring can do a great deal of internal damage. Maybe we should think about letting our children take *us* for walks instead of the other way around. Kids seem much more inclined to locate the fingerprints of God in all the smudges of the world; our job is to help them navigate.

During this inward reflection, there is a simultaneous outward reaction. We realize that we are much smaller than we thought. Standing on the edge of a high cliff makes us go weak in the knees. Paddling a raft over a raging gush of water creates a sweat that rivals the rapids. We recoil upon encountering an unexpected flame, and staring at a perfectly blue sky produces a desire to soar away from the anchor of gravity. Imagine what would happen if you were there with your child in such moments, holding her hand when she felt she was about to fall, wrapping your arms around her when the waters seemed too intense, snatching her away to a safe distance from the flames, lifting her up on your shoulders to encourage her to soar. Whether we do this literally or metaphorically, isn't this what parenting is all about?

Yes . . . and more.

There is a third, more conscious component of our response to beauty. People of every religious persuasion can appreciate the beauty of nature, but it is the unique experience of Christians to turn their gaze upward from creation to the Creator, and the unique opportunity of Christian parents to inspire an upward gaze in their children. Many religions suggest that an intelligent designer set the world in motion and then left it to fend for itself. But we believe that Jesus Christ became one of us to let us know that God is very actively restoring creation to an undistorted state. He hasn't left us alone but continues to interact with us. He is the onstage talent and the writer/director behind the scenes of the great history that is *his story*. "For from him and through him and to him are all things. To him be the glory forever! Amen" (Romans 11:36).

This has tremendous application to our parenting, from strategically planned moments to the spontaneous lessons we encounter along the way. Those who are alive to beauty—in music, art, nature, and people—are better prepared to experience the divine than those who do not know how to *wonder*.

Your child is created in the image of the most creative being in the universe. The fact that God invented colors offers great insight into what he must be like. He could have made everything gray. Aren't you glad he didn't? Perhaps we should reconsider allowing our children to paint the walls! After all, stuff is just stuff. Our children are precious reflections of a perfect Artist, and they become more like him as they express the creativity he wired into them. God is orderly; he is also wildly and extravagantly creative!

See that sky? Hear that thunder? Smell that salty sea air? This is not the work of Mother Nature! This is the work of Father Creator! Nature doesn't sustain itself—it is sustained by the One who spoke it into existence: "For by him all things were created. . . . He is before all things, and in him all things hold together" (Colossians 1:16-17).

This is why we must always point children to the God behind the colors. At each order of magnitude, creation speaks of God's boundless and surprising imagination. It tells of his enjoyment in the poetic juxtaposition of apparently disparate things. It sings of how he delights in surprise. It shouts of his craftsmanship and his ability to structure new levels of meaning and elegance into anything. It roars of the mystery of his existence, from our inability to fully grasp the structure and production of DNA to the appearance of a new star or planet.

As we humans pursue the next thing that we can name after ourselves, we find more and more holes that need filling. The lead character in *Alice in Wonderland* finds that things get "curiouser and curiouser" the further along you go. Similarly we realize that "the heavens declare the glory of God; the skies proclaim the work of his hands. Day after day they pour forth speech; night after night they display knowledge. There is no speech or language where their voice is not heard" (Psalm 19:1-3).

OVERPOWERING THE DISTORTION

What about ugliness? Whether hurricanes wipe out coastal cities or personal tragedies knock the wind out of our sails, ugliness is a reality in our fallen world. We are sometimes forced to live in the wake of destruction. If God created the world, why do some things in it repulse us? It is easy to understand what we might learn about God from beauty, but what do we learn about him when we observe ugliness? Perhaps more importantly, how can we preserve the innocence of our children while helping them to navigate the undeniable presence of evil in our world?

Imagine a very important man who has a message to communicate. He stands on a stage to share a vitally important point to a large group of people. Meanwhile, his sound technician is dared by a friend to purposely turn a knob in the wrong direction. As the speaker begins to talk, the sound technician acts on the dare and causes tremendous feedback and distortion in the room. Though the speaker's message is of significant value to the people, the audience cannot understand anything because someone is interfering with the sound. As a result, an important message is lost on a crowd whose ears are ringing.

A mother in the audience needs this important information, so she takes her child by the hand and leads her closer to the stage. By drawing nearer to the speaker, mother and daughter are able to hear the message. The distortion is still loud and hearing remains difficult, but as they lean in, the vital words come through.

Just as we must expose our children to the beauty in the world, it is also our duty to teach them about its ugliness and not shield them from it in the naive hope of protecting them. That approach is destined to fail because sooner or later they will encounter the destructive forces at work in our world. If we've painted an unrealistic picture of a world in which nothing exists but unicorns and happily-ever-after endings, our children will be more likely to discount everything else we've told them when they are confronted with real ugliness.

We are not suggesting that you compromise your children's innocence. Rather, your task is to equip them to deal with the fact that life contains cruelty and destruction.[5] As a parent, you are obligated to teach your son about leashing the dog in the backyard, and you'll have to tell him why—so the dog doesn't get run over by a car. At some point your daughter may ask about world events, and you'll need to give her a simple, filtered explanation of war and terrorism in our world. Christian parents can do this against the background of a beautifully created order, with the consolation that there is a life-changing message behind the static.

THE BEAUTIFUL SIDE OF UGLINESS

Because of God's redemptive character, even the worst distortion can be reshaped into something beautiful. Nothing is so badly damaged that it cannot be redeemed. Christianity is more realistic and optimistic about the potential of human nature than any other belief system. It allows us to recognize dignity in the midst of depravity because God believed we were so important that he paid for our lives with his. On a practical level, this is the backstory that we can teach our children as we direct their gaze toward a butterfly emerging from a cocoon or a wildflower growing out of ashes.

Along these lines, the Bible gives us some interesting facts about God's sovereignty over our distorted world and his plans for its future:

> Then I saw a new heaven and a new earth, for the first heaven and the first earth had passed away, and there was no longer any sea. I saw the Holy City, the new Jerusalem, coming down out of

heaven from God, prepared as a bride beautifully dressed for her husband. And I heard a loud voice from the throne saying, "Now the dwelling of God is with men, and he will live with them. They will be his people, and God himself will be with them and be their God. He will wipe every tear from their eyes. There will be no more death or mourning or crying or pain, for the old order of things has passed away."

He who was seated on the throne said, "I am making everything new!" Then he said, "Write this down, for these words are trustworthy and true." (Revelation 21:1-5)

Jesus once said, "The thief comes only to steal and kill and destroy; I have come that they may have life, and have it to the full" (John 10:10). This means that God forms us, Satan *de*forms us, and Christ *trans*forms us.

God formed us from the dust of the earth and breathed life into us. We were created in his image and were meant to grow up and become like him—to view our world the way he views it and to treat others the way he has treated us. We were placed in a beautiful garden, given meaningful work, and offered the chance of eternal life with no frustration, pain, or anxiety.

We do not live in such a world now. Instead, we live in a broken world, in which things are upside down. Everywhere we look, we see the beauty of God's creation vandalized by the ugliness of sin. The whole creation groans under the weight of the Curse because we listened to the dares of our enemy and chose to leave God's wisdom behind.

But that is not the end of the story. Jesus Christ became like us so that we could become like him. He offers us redemption from the Curse, purpose behind the pain we encounter, and the hope of eternity with him in a place of endless beauty.

Though Christ has offered us this abundant life, our enemy remains diligent in obscuring the message that might lead us back toward God. Satan seeks to destroy all the beauty that God has left us as a reminder of his glory and affectionate creativity, for fear that we will see beyond the creation to its Creator. Satan actively unravels the beauty of innocence and intimacy. Satan cannot mimic God's creativity, but he can spray-paint over its beauty.

How is it that we can be so duped when the obvious choice is to accept God's gracious offer? What makes us settle for ugliness when beauty is available? C. S. Lewis suggests that it is because our imaginations are feeble. He says, "We are half-hearted creatures, fooling about with drink and sex and ambition when infinite joy is offered us, like an ignorant child who wants to go on making mud pies in a slum because he cannot imagine what is meant by the offer of a holiday at the sea."[6]

Perhaps we are ignorant and short on imagination. But what drives us to play in the mud? What are we seeking?

GOD-SHAPED HOLES

Perhaps it goes back to Pascal's concept of the God-shaped hole in all of us. What was intended to drive us toward God often drives us to seek cheap substitutes and to settle for ugliness even when beauty is freely available. Our children burst out of their supposed innocence by making choices that run contrary to everything good we've taught them. What in the world are they pursuing? Presumably they are seeking the satisfaction that God created them to enjoy. The problem may or may not be where they are seeking that satisfaction. God may be found in mud as much as in sand and sea. The problem is deeper than that, rooted squarely in our fallen nature.

Thomas Dubay suggests that the problem is not in what we seek or where we seek it, but with the part of ourselves with which we do the seeking. He writes, "While the beautiful appeals to what is noble, lofty, and sublime in man, the ugly, when it attracts at all, appeals to what is selfish, wretched, squalid, and sordid."[7] Thus, settling for ugliness instead of pursuing beauty reveals our lack of transformation.

God is creative; Satan is destructive. We reflect the *imago Dei* when we create and are drawn towards creativity; we reflect our fallenness when we destroy and are attracted to destructiveness.

Perhaps the rubbernecking we do when there's an accident on the highway is further evidence of our fallen nature.

The word *ugly* rarely shows up in the Bible. A rare instance occurs in Revelation 16:2: "The first angel went and poured out his bowl on the land, and ugly and painful sores broke out on the people who had the mark of the beast and worshiped his image."

In other translations, the word *noisome* or *loathsome* is used instead of *ugly,* but in all cases the root Greek word is *kakos.* This word means "of a bad nature" or "not such as it ought to be." At its core, ugliness is anything that isn't the way it's supposed to be. Things, life, and people are supposed to be beautiful. So are relationships, churches, and societies. Unfortunately, that's not the world in which we live. [8]

In the movie *Grand Canyon,* an attorney gets stuck in a traffic jam. He tries to get around it by taking side streets, but his car breaks down in the worst of all possible neighborhoods. He manages to call a tow truck, but before it arrives, the attorney finds himself surrounded by a menacing gang. Just as things are about to get ugly, the tow truck driver shows up. As he assists the attorney, the gang members protest until the driver takes their leader aside and tells him, "Man, the world ain't supposed to work like this. Maybe you don't know that, but this ain't the way it's supposed to be. I'm supposed to be able to do my job without askin' you if I can. And that dude is supposed to be able to wait with his car without you rippin' him off. Everything's supposed to be different than what it is here."

In other words, this situation is ugly. Our world is ugly, and so are we. Again, that's not the whole truth about us, but it is certainly part of the truth. Until we are redeemed and restored, this ugliness haunts even our best days with the looming specter of our inevitable destruction.

We are ugly when we act in a way that is inconsistent with who we really are. This is an incredible insight for parenting. When children make ugly choices, we can remind them that we know deep down that this isn't who they really are. It's certainly not who they were made to be, who they can be, or who they should be. Whether it is a first offense or a pattern of rebellion, it is a teaching opportunity we should not ignore.

This raises a question: Beyond your bias as a parent and what you see purely through human eyes, how beautiful are your children . . . *really?* Do they see it, or is their view of themselves defined by secular standards?

RE-IMAGINE

Imagine what an unfallen world might be like. Don't get lost in Sunday school pictures of Adam and Eve. Rather, picture the world you live in right now as completely healed. No longer would we live in the dimly lit existence of brokenness, but we would fully know ourselves and be fully known.[9] Instead of seeing glimpses of beautiful things, we would encounter the transcendence of the Creator in everything and everyone we experience, for there would be no separation between humankind and God.[10] The joyful reunion of loved ones who had trusted in Jesus would last for all eternity.[11]

Here's the part that's really hard for us to imagine: That picture, an unfallen world, exists right now. It's the real world that is emerging beneath this one, and we are called to focus on it.[12] Even the ugliness of wars, natural disasters, and famine are somehow serving God's purposes so that his beauty might one day be revealed in its fullness.[13] That which is unseen is more real than that which we've laid eyes on.[14] "That other place" is actually "this place" as it really is.

For now, we live in the "shadowlands," where all things—good and bad—reveal to all humankind the powerful and creative chiseling of God.[15] Nature is beautiful because it is a reflection of God. G. K. Chesterton writes:

> Because children have abounding vitality, because they are in spirit fierce and free, therefore they want things repeated and unchanged. They always say, Do it again; and the grown-up person does it again until he is nearly dead. For grown-up people are not strong enough to exult in monotony. But perhaps God is strong enough. . . . It is possible that God says every morning, Do it again, to the sun; and every evening, Do it again, to the moon. It may not

be automatic necessity that makes all daisies alike: it may be that God makes every daisy separately, but has never got tired of making them. It may be that He has the eternal appetite of infancy; for we have sinned and grown old, and our Father is younger than we.[16]

Do it again! If we perceive the connection between the magnificent splendor of creation and the Creator and Sustainer behind it all, then beauty will still be wrapped up with longing. We will beg God to "do it again" because the Beautiful One can do so.

We long to be in a mountaintop cabin overlooking trees and rivers. We long for spring to come. We long to see our loved ones. We long to hear our child's happy laugh. We may not always be aware of it, but nature makes us long for things. There is a deep longing for God within the human heart. The psalmist says, "As the deer pants for streams of water, so my soul pants for you, O God" (Psalm 42:1).

All pleasures come from God's hands. All beauty emerges from his creativity.[17] The correlation between our desires and our quest for beauty confirms that there is something beyond us that we crave. Because deep down we really are created in God's image, then it follows that everything he has created speaks of his desire to reconnect with us. From the tiniest blade of grass to the largest star in the sky, God has been telling a story that he longs for us to be a part of.[18] There's an elegant unity in how the complex and the simple hint at the harmonious order of an intelligent designer. In this way, the Lord uses our built-in appreciation of the natural world to encourage us toward the supernatural.

We can teach this beauty to children by exploring nature with them firsthand. We can start with the microscopic and move to galaxies. We can examine shells, flowers, plants, and water. We can use microscopes, binoculars, and telescopes. We can look at Renaissance art and listen to classical music. We can look at images of animals on the Internet, and we can examine images found in great poetry and the lyrics of great songs.

We can enter nature with our children, taking the time required to really experience something breathtaking. We can use these opportunities to talk about how God created all things. Explore the details and the amazing way things work, from the design of beetles to the form and function the Creator gave them for moving about. If we lay a foundation for our children to be good "finders," we may just learn something new ourselves.

Remember that this is more than a biology lesson or an art class. C. S. Lewis called beauty the "patches of godlight on the woodlands of our experience."[19] Your task is to take advantage of these opportunities to lead your children to Jesus. Recent studies have shown that nearly half of Americans who accept Jesus Christ as their Savior do so before reaching the age of thirteen, and half of them are led to Christ by their parents.[20] The same survey also shows that people who become Christians before their teen years are more likely than other Christians to remain absolutely committed to Christianity. Shouldn't we make the most of this opportunity?

Consider the beauty of the Bible and what it tells us about God. It contains the inspirational true stories of men, women, and children over thousands of years who have interacted with God, and it is a living and active voice in our lives today.[21] We can look at Daniel's stunning commitment to God; we can make our way through the book of Proverbs; we can study the first five books of the Bible and allow the law to provide a structure for life as it was intended to be. For the best picture of a beautiful life, look at Jesus. Nature is one expression of God's beauty, but Jesus is its prime representation.[22]

Pray that God will catch you and your family off guard with his beauty and that he will help you slow down enough to enjoy it. Enjoy the inward, outward, and upward journey together. It may lead your children to receive Jesus Christ as their Savior, and it will provide them with a foundation for seeking him for the rest of their lives.

That is a beautiful thing.

part 4
What We Do

*In churches, we hear a lot about faith,
hope, and love. We hear the words so
much that they may have lost their meaning
for us. Still, we remember that faith is real
and tangible. Genuine faith is shown in
action. Our behavior rather than our closely
held beliefs will convince our children that
we are people they want to emulate.
When we demonstrate our faith in the
goodness of God, especially amid difficult
circumstances, our children will learn that
hope stems from an eternal perspective.
The last chapter in this section deals with
the Christian foundations that motivate our
love for all people. By combining this
understanding of people as God's precious
creatures with a faith that serves others and
a hope that God's kingdom will prevail, we
can provide our children with a model of
true Christianity that they can follow their
entire lives.*

"Are we there yet?" That's a question all kids ask any time they take a car trip. It's not a deep philosophical question, but it's universal. There seems to be an inverse correlation between the length of the journey and the time lapse between your departure and the first time they ask the question. They ask it early and often, and when you finally answer, they ask you again: "Are we there yet?"

Do you ever wonder who might have been the first person to ask that question? Was it Abraham's wife, Sarah? Her husband came to her one day and told her to pack everything up because this Yahweh character had told him to go somewhere. She hadn't dealt with Yahweh before, and she had no idea what to expect. She must have asked Abraham, "Where are we going?"

"I don't know," he said, "but Yahweh said he would tell me when we get there."

How long do you suppose Sarah waited, once they were under way, before she asked him, "Are we there yet?"

The truth about us is not so different. God has called us, and often we don't know exactly where we're going or how long the trip might take. We wander around in the desert and get tired. We get cranky. We worry that we might not ever make it. Then we worry that the whole thing is some kind of practical joke. Maybe we didn't get the message right. Maybe, in the words of that great explorer Bugs Bunny, we should have turned left at Albuquerque. It doesn't take long before we start asking God, "Are we there yet?"

Life isn't a sprint; it's a marathon. It requires patience, endurance, and determination. God calls us to a life that compels us to leave behind everything comfortable—everything we have known—to venture into the unknown on a great adventure of faith. It matters that we begin well, and it matters even more that we finish well. But what does finishing well look like? What is this thing called faith, anyway? And how do faith-filled parents raise their kids?

The writer of Hebrews tells us, "Faith is the substance of things hoped for, the evidence of things not seen" (Hebrews 11:1, NKJV). According to this verse, faith is substantial. It is evidence that offers tangible proof of something invisible. In other words, faith is more than simply belief; it is belief that stirs some kind of activity, often the kind that changes the world forever.

Faith like that can cause us to do crazy things. Faith will make a man build a boat because God said that it would rain sometime soon and wouldn't stop for more than a month. Faith will make a man leave his hometown behind with nothing but an unseen God to guide him. Faith will make a married couple start trying to have a baby after all their friends have retired and moved to Florida. Faith will make a mother hide her baby in a basket and place it in the river or a fugitive return home and face down the most powerful man in the world. Faith will make a young boy confront a giant, a lone prophet challenge hundreds of rivals at Mount Carmel, and a man risk a night in the lions' den rather than stop praying. Faith will make a young girl accept the message of an angel about a miraculous birth. Faith will make a ragtag group of uneducated men turn the Roman Empire and the rest of the world upside down.

Faith surrenders to the leadership of the Holy Spirit, even though he refuses to be tamed and usually reveals the details of his plan on a strictly need-to-know basis. Like the Lion Aslan, the Holy Spirit is good, but he's far from safe. He blows people wherever he wants to, descending like a dove one day and falling like tongues of fire the next.[1] He spoke through the prophets.[2] He led Jesus to the desert to be tempted and anointed Jesus so he could preach and heal.[3] He leads us into all truth and speaks directly to our consciences to convict us when we've done wrong.[4] He settles our minds and gives us life and peace.[5] He keeps us from sin and builds Christlike character in us.[6] He is our Counselor and pours God's love into our hearts.[7] He inspires our dreams and gives us the visions that lead to the works of faith for which we were created.[8] He marks those who belong to God.[9]

The Holy Spirit gives us the power to resist sin and live godly lives,[10] but don't think that he's safe. He's not. He's not nearly as interested in our comfort levels as in our character development, and shaping our character is often a remarkably painful process for us. Because he's not safe and he asks us to do painful, character-shaping things, maybe we ought to think twice before inviting him into our lives. He's not comfortable to live with. He often takes us out of our comfort zones and makes us acknowledge that we can't accomplish on our own what we're called to do.

Parenting is a prime example of that. The Holy Spirit knows where he's going, and he knows the deepest thoughts of God,[11] but to us he can look like an aimless wanderer.[12] He's in us and we're in him. We can't sneak off without his noticing, and he's not going to leave us alone. When we go where he says, he often leads us into situations that are decidedly unsafe (lions' dens, fiery furnaces, shipwrecks).

The Holy Spirit is the Helper Jesus left for us, and if we want to belong to God, we must live closer than side by side with this apparently aimless, unpredictable Spirit. Jesus said of him, "The wind blows wherever it pleases. You hear its sound, but you cannot tell where it comes from or where it is going. So it is with everyone born of the Spirit" (John 3:8).

The Bible says that we're not to be tossed here and there by every "wind of teaching" (Ephesians 4:14), but by following the Holy Spirit, sometimes it will appear to others that we have lost our sense of direction. Being blown around by God is often the mark of those "born of the Spirit." It is with some trepidation that we as believers bear the mark of the One whom no one can catch and whose course no one can plot. But bear it we must, because though he's a wanderer, we will never arrive without him.[13]

We are primarily a purpose-driven rather than a goal-oriented people because we can't see what we seek. As God called Abraham and Jesus
called his disciples, they also call us to follow the leading of the Holy
Spirit.

Are we there yet?

No, we're not there yet; but we're closer than we've ever been
because all our travels form the character of Christ in us, and he is our
ultimate destination. The world watches as we leave our tents in the
desert and our nets by the sea in dogged pursuit of the One who has
promised never to leave us or forsake us. We make an impact wherever
we are led because of the One who leads us. He alone is the purpose of
life, and *toward him* is the only direction. Those who live this way are on
the road to becoming heroes of faith. We are Abraham's children.

> Abraham's faith [was] characterized not by adherence to any
> law or any set of correct behaviors or any institution or may-God-
> help-me creeds or confessions, but by complete trust in God. . . .
> [Our] leap of faith comes with great fear and trembling, because
> God's call to Abram is a call to leave what is familiar and to go to
> a new place that God will show him when he gets there.[14]

A journey without a map? Leaving security with only the hope
of something more secure?[15] That doesn't sound like good parenting.
Shouldn't we rather opt for protecting our children, raising them un-
stained by the world so they can go out later . . . when they're older . . .
when we don't have to worry so much?

NOAH AND JONAH: A TALE OF TWO SAILORS

Along with Abraham, Noah is also in the Hebrews 11 "hall of faith." It
was really fun to learn his story in kindergarten—all those animals and
that great big boat. If we had a really creative Bible teacher, we got more
than just a flannel-board image. Maybe we actually got to play in the
water and float the boat, or maybe we played "pin the animal in the ark."
Even those with limited Sunday school experience are familiar with the

story of Noah and the Flood. Perhaps our familiarity with the story makes us realize that it's supposed to be our story. If we're going to be faithful, we think, we must be like Noah. So we hide ourselves in an ark and try to float away from this terrible world.

Maybe you haven't noticed, but there hasn't been a global flood lately, and there's not going to be one anytime soon. We're not called to be like Noah and his family, hidden away in a boat and cut off from the people God plans to destroy. Right now we're more like Jonah. We're called to go to people and lovingly warn them.

The problem is that we may be too much like Jonah. We don't much like the people we're supposed to save, and though we would never say this, we don't really want to see them rescued. Do we really want hostile atheists who ridicule Christianity to receive the grace and mercy of God? Wouldn't we much rather see them be surprised on the last day? We want people who oppose our values to get what they've got coming to them. We want them to get justice while we receive mercy.

In Micah 6:8, we're told to "love mercy." As Gary Thomas points out, "People who love mercy are not thankful merely for the mercy *they* have received; those who love mercy are also eager to show mercy to *others*."[16]

Christians must resist the temptation to withdraw from society. We must actively engage and influence our culture.[17] If God sent us into the world to do the kinds of things Jesus did (and even greater things![18]), we ought to be doing them out where the world can see. If the Holy Spirit is renewing our minds,[19] then our ideas matter and we ought to be making them heard in the marketplace. Our faith must be lived in public, not in "Christian ghettos." Communities where only Christians were allowed would not bring light to the rest of the world. They also would not represent the nomadic Holy Spirit very well.

What makes us feel obligated to pull out of society, hole up, hide away, and bring our kids with us? Could it be that we lack the faith to roll up our sleeves, risk being uncomfortable, and get involved with the people Jesus loved so much that he died to save them? Perhaps that's what's behind all the fearful messages Christians propagate, all the crazy e-mail hoaxes we forward, and all the Chicken Little "the sky is falling!" books we write.

The world is not a safe place for Christians. The light of the gospel has broken into this world, but it is still a dangerous, hostile place that often refuses to treat us kindly. God sent his Son into a perilous world, and he calls us to do the same with our children.

You can hear Christian radio stations every day claiming to be "safe for the whole family." We know what they mean, but who in the world ever said that Christianity was supposed to be safe? Jesus said the exact opposite. He said we shouldn't be surprised if our faith gets us in trouble. His followers always seem to be getting into dangerous and disturbing situations. The Bible shows God constantly calling people out of safety into areas of danger and risk, where faith is their survival kit.

Maybe one of the best things we can do as parents is to ask ourselves, "What am I doing that requires a large amount of faith? Is there any area of my life in which I'm taking risks for God?" If there isn't, you might need to consider what your inactivity is communicating to your kids about your level of faith in God and your attitude about what he wants to accomplish through you in this world.

If we teach our kids that safety is the highest virtue, we will fail to teach them that certain things are worth risking our safety for. Safety is good—unless it replaces godliness as the ultimate goal for our children.

FACING FORWARD

According to Jesus, real faith—trusting God no matter how upside down things appear—moves mountains. Faith should move *us* as well—off of our sofas, out from in front of our television screens and computer monitors, out of our comfortable suburban neighborhoods, and into the world that is not always safe for the whole family.

Faith asks us to face forward rather than to look back with false nostalgia for the good old days. Part of being a faithful person is facing the future with the courageous tenacity to persevere in doing what God has called us to do. Abraham did not look in the rearview mirror at what he had left behind. Instead, "He was looking forward to the city with foundations, whose architect and builder is God" (Hebrews 11:10). In other words, he was looking for the fulfillment of God's promise.

"The city" is a biblical image for the community that God has planned for humans. He intends that people should be rightly related to God and to one another. This community is characterized by love, joy, peace, and patience. Kindness is the norm there, and generosity comes as easily as breathing. God's community lives at the crossroads of civilization so that the whole world will know what his people look like. Such a community stands out like a city set on a hill, shining its light into the surrounding darkness as a witness to a watching world that wants to be included.

Abraham didn't know that he would die before he ever saw that community come to fruition. It didn't matter. God had given him a vision, and Abraham was not going to stop seeking it.

If we know we won't see something in this lifetime, we often prefer to just grit our teeth and endure this world until we die and go to heaven. We sing, "Farther along we'll know all about it. Farther along we'll understand why," and we interpret those words to mean that because we won't understand it all until then, we should not ask too many questions now. Let's not work too hard. Instead, let's just talk about how great it will be to get there, and let's never lift a finger to make this dark world a brighter place.

Notice how Jesus instructs us to pray in his model prayer. He says, "Your kingdom come, your will be done *on earth as it is in heaven"* (Matthew 6:10, emphasis added). He does not tell us to pray, "God, take us from down here to up there." He tells us to ask God to bring "up there" down here. Then he instructs us in actively playing our part by living in absolute and fearless trust, by practicing forgiveness, and by building our lives on God's wise principles.

Whether because of fear, apathy, or a desire to seek comfort and safety rather than transformation and character, the truth is that too many Christians have withdrawn from society and culture. Rather than being the redemptive agents God desires us to be, we have left the world on its own as we build our Christian ghettos and refuse to engage those whom Christ loves.

THE SPIRIT AND MR. WILBERFORCE

It isn't always that way. The history of Christianity (and present-day Christianity, for that matter) is rich with people who have believed that God called them to work toward creating his community in this world. These people have fought for justice and compassion and have given their lives to advancing God's kingdom and fulfilling his purposes. Courageous men and women of faith have followed the lead of God's Spirit, regardless of the cost.

William Wilberforce was born in 1759 to a family of merchants in Hull, England. Because he was frequently sick, he grew to be just over five feet tall. He was terribly nearsighted and not very strong, but what he lacked in physical strength, he more than made up for with charm, a clear mind, articulate speech, and the added benefits of wealth and a high social status. His mother sent him to good schools and made sure that he attended the right social events. His aunt, with whom he lived briefly, was a Christian and a friend of the great preacher George Whitefield, but William's mother took pains to make sure that he would not be overcome by "religious enthusiasm." [20] And so he was not. He lived a comfortable life and made a lot of friends, among them William Pitt, who would later become prime minister.

In 1780, when Wilberforce was twenty-one, he was elected to the House of Commons. He was popular and had a goal in mind: to become prime minister. Though he was small and prone to illness, he was so sharp and eloquent that he won the respect of the people he represented and of the people with whom he worked. But he had no sense of destiny. He pursued his political ambitions, content to advance his personal agenda as far as he could.

That would change. In 1785, after reading Philip Doddridge's book called *The Rise and Progress of Religion in the Soul,* Wilberforce experienced a crisis of faith. He realized that, in spite of his religious upbringing, he had never really committed himself to the life of faith that he professed. He wrote in his journal, "The deep guilt and black ingratitude of my past life forced itself on me in the strongest colours, and I condemned myself for having wasted precious time and opportunities and talents." [21]

He considered that using those talents for Christian service might require him to leave public service, but John Newton (writer of the hymn *Amazing Grace*), a former slave trader who had become a Christian minister, convinced him otherwise. Wilberforce said of their first meeting that he had "ten thousand doubts" about going to see Newton; it could have been political suicide. He walked around the block twice before he could muster up the courage to knock on Newton's door. To his astonishment, Newton urged him not to withdraw from public life but to remain active in Parliament, where he could make a positive moral difference in the world. Two years after their initial meeting, Newton wrote to Wilberforce: "It is hoped and believed that the Lord has raised you up for the good of His church and for the good of the nation." [22]

Wilberforce began to use his political influence to call the people of his class to a higher moral standard of living. Immorality and inaction were rampant in British high society, even among those who claimed to be Christians. He wrote a book admonishing the British elite to come back to their faith, and it sold well for more than forty years. [23] He later wrote another book called *Practical Christianity*. His voice became "the conscience of Parliament."

His reputation as a man of conviction and morality prompted Sir Charles Middleton, comptroller of the British Navy and also a Christian, to confide in him regarding something terrible he had witnessed. Middleton's disclosure would impel Wilberforce toward what would become his life's work. Once, upon boarding a French slave ship in the West Indies, Middleton witnessed the slave trade firsthand. He saw men and women stripped of the dignity they deserved as humans created in the likeness of God. He was convinced that this could not be part of God's plan. Middleton asked Wilberforce to become the voice for abolition in Parliament.

Although Wilberforce believed himself to be unequal to the task, he did not refuse. He set out to prove that ending the slave trade was a moral imperative. Even today we can trace the demise of the worldwide slave trade back to this one man.

Historians tell us that the first Englishman to transport slaves from Africa to the New World was probably Sir John Hawkins, in 1562. He captured people in Sierra Leone and sold them to Spanish settlers in the Caribbean. When Queen Elizabeth I heard about it, she was outraged, declaring the slave trade to be detestable and predicting that it would "call down the vengeance of Heaven upon the undertakers."

Once she saw how profitable the business was, however, her greed got the best of her. Two years later, she rented Hawkins a seven-hundred-ton ship (ironically named the *Jesus of Lubeck*) for his next voyage. Eventually more than eleven million people would be shipped across the Atlantic to a life of slavery.

Conditions on slave ships were grossly inhumane. Slaves were routinely branded like cattle, shackled together, and packed so tightly into a ship's hull that each had a space approximately sixteen inches wide and six feet long. There was so little oxygen below deck that it was often hard to keep candles burning. There was no light or sanitation, and disease was rampant. Food was scarce, and violence was plentiful. Many people died en route and were either thrown overboard or left shackled to the others. Those who survived had to wonder what their survival was worth. They continued to live, but they were deprived of the most basic human rights. They were regarded as property, and not very valuable property at that.

In 1781, the slave ship *Zong*, under the command of Luke Collingwood, left the coast of Africa for Jamaica with 133 slaves, far more than the ship had room for. When they arrived in Jamaica, many of the slaves were near death. What happened next is almost unimaginable. Collingwood told his crew that if the slaves died a natural death, he and the men would be held financially responsible for letting them die. But if the slaves were thrown overboard while still alive—say, for the sake of the crew's safety—then their insurance would have to cover the financial loss. All 133 slaves were thrown overboard.

Upon his return, Collingwood attempted to collect the full value of the murdered slaves from his insurers. When the truth of his actions was revealed, his lawyers defended what he had done. After all, they claimed, the slaves weren't to be viewed as people. They were cargo. Instead of being appalled by this inhumanity, the judge agreed with them, saying that what they had done was the equivalent of jettisoning horses.

Then William Wilberforce arrived on the scene.

When Wilberforce decided to take on slavery, it occupied a place in the British economy roughly equivalent to the national defense industry in the United States today. This didn't stop Wilberforce. Though Parliament stubbornly refused his reforms for twenty years, it eventually surrendered to his powerful, passionate cry for equality among all humans. His tenacious endurance is proof positive that one man's faith *can* make a difference in the world.

PURPOSE-DRIVEN BUT NOT ALONE

What gave Wilberforce such tenacity? What prompted this popular man to take such an unpopular stance? Why in the world would a man of means with political aspirations sabotage his chances of becoming the most powerful man in England?

The answer is simple: Wilberforce was a Christian, and Christians are purpose-driven rather than simply goal-oriented. He was following in the footsteps of others who were led by the roving Spirit, those who left nets, tents, and reputations to travel with the only One who knows the way to God and who always leaves change in his wake. Wilberforce jettisoned his aspirations for political prestige and endured heavy persecution as he pursued an invisible city whose architect and builder is God.

When Wilberforce spoke about the horrors of slavery, he stood with Moses, Amos, Micah, and all people of faith who had gone before him. He was on a "not there yet" journey toward the community of God's kingdom. He was not alone because he was surrounded by a "great cloud of witnesses" (Hebrews 12:1). He was walking in the power of the Spirit, and if God was for him, who could be against him?

Oddly, the men who opposed Wilberforce in Parliament considered themselves Christians too. Wilberforce realized, however, that a personal pronouncement of faith needs some corroborating evidence. When faith is real, it is always intertwined with action. As the Bible says:

> What good is it, my brothers, if a man claims to have faith but has no deeds? Can such faith save him? Suppose a brother or sister is without clothes and daily food. If one of you says to him, "Go, I wish you well; keep warm and well fed," but does nothing about his physical needs, what good is it? In the same way, faith by itself, if it is not accompanied by action, is dead.
>
> But someone will say, "You have faith; I have deeds."
>
> Show me your faith without deeds, and I will show you my faith by what I do. (James 2:14-18)

Wilberforce knew that he couldn't affirm the Bible and treat African people as property. Jesus told those who wanted to be his followers to love their neighbors as they loved themselves, and Wilberforce recognized that loving his neighbors could not mean standing idly by while fellow human beings were abused and enslaved. If he really had faith in Christ, he must demonstrate that faith by speaking for a people who had no voice.

INTO THE WORLD

What does this have to do with us as parents? It means we cannot elevate the value of our own family's comfort and safety and then sit idly by while fellow human beings are abused and enslaved. What good does it do to isolate our families from unbelievers when our brothers and sisters in church hate those they're called to love? What is accomplished by withdrawal from a world we're called to serve? If you really have faith in Christ, you must demonstrate it by faithful action in the here and now, in the land of "not yet."

Politics can be an ugly business. Public schools can be dangerous. Boardrooms on Wall Street and break rooms at the local plant hear more than their fair share of false, evil, and ugly language. Why would a Christian be caught dead in those arenas?

Because that's where Jesus would be.

The influence, ideas, and input of Christians are desperately needed in those places. If Christians withdraw from politics, public schools, boardrooms, and break rooms, how will these places ever be redeemed? We will never shape public policy with biblical values or alter corrupt systems to protect the weak and vulnerable if we have withdrawn from the world. We should admit that the primary reason for our withdrawal is that we lack serious and substantive faith in the power of the gospel to transform people's hearts and minds. And then we should bolster our faith and get back out there.

Jesus told his followers to go into the world—not to be corrupted by it, but to influence it by being salt, light, and leaven. He told his followers to get off the sidelines and get involved in helping others in need.

Wilberforce knew that to really demonstrate his faith, he had to do more than just attend church and have personal devotions. The veracity of his claim to faith would be established by his actively engaging the culture around him and working with God to overthrow corrupt systems.

As parents, we must understand that same thing. You may not think that your children are paying attention to you. You may think that you have to yell, jump up and down, and light the coffee table on fire to get them to listen. But trust us: Your kids are watching and listening. They hear your racial jokes. They see you drive past the woman having car trouble at the side of the road. They know when you're speeding, and they learn from you how to slow down when the police officer is parked in the median. They observe how you treat your spouse and what you say about the preacher at lunch on Sunday after church.

In his musical *Into the Woods,* Stephen Sondheim wrote, "Children may not obey, but children will listen." What do your children hear when they listen to you? What do they learn from what you do?

After William Wilberforce recommitted his life to Christ at age twenty-five, his initial thought was to retire from politics and become an ordained minister. If Newton hadn't convinced him not to retreat from public life, he probably would have done so. Who knows where we might be now if he had? Like many Christians today, he thought there was a difference between "spiritual" things and "secular" things. He thought at first that the only people who used their minds and their influence for Christian good were preachers. His mind was changed by John Newton. Who will change ours?

SHOOTING OURSELVES IN THE FOOT

How should we live as parents? We should be informed about the pressing issues of our day. We should vote according to our conscience for leaders with godly character and commitments. We should write intelligent letters to editors. We should raise up intellectual leaders for the next generation. We should allow our faith to drive us into the world as ambassadors of Christ (2 Corinthians 5:20), determined to leave the world better than we found it. We must push back the forces of darkness and brighten our corner of the world with the light of God's presence.

That's what faith does, and that's how faith will empower our parenting.

Unfortunately, we are often our own worst enemies. We destroy our credibility by spouting half-baked conspiracy theories and forwarding ridiculous e-mail hoaxes. The impression we give to thinking non-Christians is that in order to become Christians, they will have to check their brains at the door. We dishonor God when we fail to love him with our minds. If we're going to engage our culture in meaningful and relevant ways, we must be prepared with facts that will stand up to scrutiny. We've got to use our heads, do our homework, and live with intellectual integrity.

Wilberforce was a gentleman, not a jerk. He didn't call people names or attack them personally. He didn't stand outside the palace of Westminster hurling nasty epithets as the legislators entered. When others attacked him, he refused to respond in kind. He maintained a sense of joy and humor. He actually seemed to care about others as much as he cared about winning an argument. Too often Christians today prove their point and win an argument, but come across as mean-spirited. A person of faith should refuse to compromise the truth, but truth must be attended by grace.

Our faith is not to be hidden or kept to ourselves. Faith is meant to be shared with others. We must get involved, and that will mean interacting with people who disagree with us and who oppose the values we cherish. In those situations, we must remember that how we interact with others matters greatly to God.

Often in our attempts to change the world, we create an "us against them" mentality that pushes people away from the gospel. We should never use tactics that bring shame and reproach upon the body of Christ. Wilberforce put it this way in a diary entry: "A man who acts from the principles I profess reflects that he is to give an account of his political conduct at the Judgment seat of Christ."

LEAVING A LEGACY OF EXCELLENCE

Some diligent scholars are working to make the works of John Newton better known.[24] The work he inspired in Wilberforce is visible every day of our lives. It took another twenty-six years to end slavery in England altogether, but it happened—three days before Wilberforce died. The American abolition movement followed, and we now see the descendants of former slaves living freely in our country.

Wilberforce's life presents a powerful testimony to the earthshattering power of one man's faith in the gospel. Why did Wilberforce act on the belief that freedom should be the inalienable right of all ethnicities? Why did he believe that human life is intrinsically valuable and that ending slavery was a moral imperative? Wilberforce fought for these things because he embraced a Christian worldview that told him, "We are not there yet, but we are here, and we must begin to expand the borders of God's kingdom where we are."

What if the best public speakers in our world all had the faith of

William Wilberforce? What if the best lawmakers, the most well-respected and sought-after thinkers in the realm of public policy, human rights, medicine, and astrophysics were all Christians? What if the most innovative and creative people on the planet—artists, musicians, architects, novelists—and the award winners in every field from journalism to graphic design were all Christians? What if every time you sought the advice or opinion of someone successful, that person turned out to be a Christian? What message would that send to a skeptical world, and how viable would arguments against the Christian faith seem against that backdrop?

Slavery still exists in our world. Millions of men, women, and children live as slaves. In Southeast Asia, boys and girls are abducted and sold every day. They are forced to work long hours in unacceptable and often cruel conditions, deprived of education, rest, and recreation. Isolated from friends and family, they are under the complete control of their owners, who often subject them to unspeakable abuse.

This is a foreign concept to many of us because slavery as a publicly supported institution was virtually destroyed, in less than one hundred years, and it all started with one man. What influence might each of us bring to bear against evil?

NOT YET BUT ONE DAY

"God is not ashamed to be called their God, for he has prepared a city for them" (Hebrews 11:16). God really has prepared a heavenly city for us. Abraham, the father of the faithful, was an alien and a stranger when he lived on this earth. He was on a pilgrimage, and he wouldn't be stopped. His whole life was one long "not there yet."

Like him, we must keep going. The faith that Jesus inspires and the Holy Spirit sustains is the faith that creates heroes such as William Wilberforce—men and women who fight for truth and justice with passionate intensity. Wilberforce is a great example of faith in action. He was also a dad. His sons and grandsons emulated his faith and became authors, reformers, and church leaders. They maintained their father's belief that the Spirit who led them to faith would also lead them to make a difference in the world.

No, we're not there yet. But it's our responsibility to make a difference right now.

There is power in a dream, especially when that dream is in sync with God's dream. God longs for justice and redemption, and he tells us that one day all the things that are wrong about our world will be set right. Dr. Martin Luther King Jr. had a dream that was powerful enough to lead people to sit in, stand up, march on, take notice, and suffer abuse for the sake of preventing further abuse.

> I have a dream today. I have a dream that one day every valley shall be exalted, every hill and mountain shall be made low, the rough places will be made plain, and the crooked places will be made straight, and the glory of the Lord shall be revealed, and all flesh shall see it together. This is our hope. This is the faith with which I return to the South. With this faith we will be able to hew out of the mountain of despair a stone of hope.[1]

King inspired leaders, recruited followers, and demanded legislative reform. He moved people, black and white, because he could envision what was true, good, and beautiful, and he refused to give up. He said that justice would one day roll down like waters, and righteousness like a mighty stream.[2] By his absolute refusal to be silenced, he forced America to deal with the error, the evil, and the ugliness of racism.

Martin Luther King Jr. was a hope-filled and inspirational leader. He was also a dad. While he was in Washington, proclaiming his dream that his children would "one day live in a nation where they [would] not be judged by the color of their skin but by the content of their character,"[3] his wife, Coretta, was caring for his four children, the youngest of whom turned five months old that day.

King left a legacy of hope for our nation and for his own family.

OF HOPE AND ENDURANCE

Young children are characteristically hopeful. The last person to stop rooting for the home team, admit defeat, or quit leading the cheers for a comeback is usually a child. Children are often incurably hopeful, optimistic, and given to great dreams.

The worst thing that could happen to your children would be for them to have their hopes crushed, their dreams dashed, and their course set toward a cynical and pessimistic adulthood. It is up to us, as Christian parents, to make sure that their dreams are encouraged, fostered, and directed, and that their hopes are set on something that can never die or be defeated.

Unfortunately, many parenting books and programs disregard this fundamental need to instill hope. We are so often focused on obedience that we may inadvertently steal hope from our children rather than channel and nurture it. Long-term studies have proven that children merely trained in obedience are less productive, less happy members of society. When parents enforce a rigid, behavior-oriented model of parenting, they "may not only run the risk of undermining a baby's capacity for trust, but unknowingly may be contributing to a disorder of the self in their child. The desired result of an exceptionally obedient child may be realized; however, the form of obedience created may actually thwart the capacity to internalize empathy, gratitude, and love." [4]

The cultivation of hope is essential to Christian endurance, whether in a child or in a grandparent. Hope gives us a rationale for the risks of faith. Hope helps us allow our children to move through the stages of faith in spite of fear and without getting stuck. Hope is not optional; it is a requirement for living the life of faith that we discussed in the last chapter. Faith without hope leads to a sense of futility, robbing us of the joy that Jesus has promised us as his followers.

Without real hope, dreams are just illusions. Dr. King would have accomplished nothing by standing before thousands and proclaiming, "I have a wish. . . ." Wishful thinking doesn't inspire momentum. Thankfully, Dr. King's motivating vision was rooted in a hope that he knew would not disappoint. He knew that he might not live to see it, but the day would come when men, women, and children from "every nation, tribe, people and language" would stand together in a place where skin color wouldn't matter (Revelation 7:9). His dream was vivid and real to him, and he worked with all his might toward seeing it realized in his lifetime.

Though our vision may differ from that of Martin Luther King Jr., our hope must be the same as his. One day God will set all wrong things right, and he is great enough to help us hew stones of hope out of our mountains of despair. One day this dream will be a reality. Perhaps we should work toward seeing it realized in *our* lifetimes.

HOPE FLOATS

"Abandon all hope, all ye who enter here." So reads the sign above the gates of hell in Dante's *Inferno*. Does hopelessness pave the way to hell? It has been said that people can endure virtually anything—loss of health, job, spouse, children, status, or the respect of friends and colleagues. People have survived these things and worse, but no one can survive the loss of hope.

Richard Wurmbrand became a Christian in 1938. His faith led him to study, and he eventually became an ordained minister of the gospel. In 1944, when the Communists gained control of his native Romania, he began ministering to his fellow Romanians and to the Russian soldiers occupying his country. When the government attempted to control the churches, he began an underground ministry.

For this faith and zeal, Wurmbrand was arrested, on his way to church, and sent to prison. Three of his years there were spent in solitary confinement in a cell thirty feet below the ground. The only time he saw other people was when they came to interrogate and torture him. Yet he was able to remember the lyrics of the song "Jesus Loves Me," even though he had no Bible to tell him so. He rewrote the words to say, "Yes, Jesus loves me, their faces tell me so." How the faces of his torturers could tell him that Jesus loved him is probably beyond most of us. Wurmbrand tells of the hopes that held him together during those years, saying, "I had a faint hope that one day I might be released."[5] He crafted sermons every night, memorized them, and preached them directly to a God he knew was there and who he hoped would save him and allow him to preach to his people again.

Wurmbrand's hope was realized when he was released in 1956. Although he was warned not to preach anymore, he resumed his work and was arrested again in 1959. This time he was sentenced to twenty-five years in prison, but he still refused to abandon hope. Or perhaps hope refused to abandon him.

In 1964, in response to mounting political pressure, he was released and given amnesty. The leaders of the underground church convinced him to leave Romania, and he spent the rest of his life traveling through Europe and the United States as a spokesman for the persecuted church. In April 1967, Wurmbrand formed an organization called Jesus to the Communist World (later named The Voice of the Martyrs), and in 1990, Richard and his wife, Sabina, returned to Romania to open a Christian printing facility and a bookstore in Bucharest. City officials donated storage space for their ministry. The space, it turns out, was at the very site where Wurmbrand had been held in solitary confinement. By the time he died in 2001, his hopes were realized beyond his wildest dreams.

How can we, by our lives, instill in our children the hope that is so essential for survival in the worst of circumstances? How do we tell our kids about hope when we hope that their faith never brings them to this kind of suffering?

As we've said before, you cannot give something away that you do not have. Unless the hope of God is *in* you, your children will never acquire it *from* you. As parents, we must constantly remember the Cross and the resurrected Savior. As we live in the shadow of the Cross and in the light of the empty tomb, we can tell our children that in this present world, dead things (such as the pet who was hit by a car) stay dead, but in the Kingdom of God, there is the promise of resurrection. The dead come back to life, and all things are made new. This hope anchors our souls, preventing us from being tossed about by our circumstances.

Only then can we tell our children stories of Jesus and of the faithful people found in our Bibles, our churches, and our communities who embody the truth of God's grace and hope. Stories about heroes of the faith help us to envision becoming great ourselves as we realize their stories could be our stories. Daniel, Deborah, Joseph, Ruth, and Hannah encourage our faith, shape our morals, and sustain our hope in what might otherwise seem like a hopeless environment or circumstance. The "great cloud of witnesses" in Hebrews 11 reminds us where we come from and how far we can go with the hope that our faith inspires.

Leonard Sweet has written eloquently about how the current generation learns. Rather than just gathering propositional truths, today's young people prefer stories that interconnect to form a larger narrative. What more perfect forum for this kind of storytelling than in Christian homes and churches? If parents and churches ignore this form of teaching, we ignore a powerful shaping force that is easily at our disposal, and we may fail to communicate altogether. Dr. Sweet says, "Cultures are symbol systems, intricate, interwoven webs of metaphors, symbols and stories. What holds the culture of the church together—the metaphors it offers, the symbols it displays, the stories it tells?" [6]

According to Sweet, today we "have lost the plot to the stories of Jesus." [7] If we care about the generation now growing up in our churches, we must find those plots again because the overarching story line gives meaning and significance to all the subplots along the way. We should arrange our teaching into stories around that plot line, and we should tell them over and over.

Along with the stories of the Bible, we should tell our children our own stories and those of faithful men and women throughout history. Susan B. Anthony, Abraham Lincoln, Sojourner Truth, Martin Luther, Florence Nightingale, Dwight Moody, and thousands of other great men and women took their faith to streets, pulpits, halls of government, and educational institutions, and left the world a little brighter for their having been here. These stories inspire the hope that one day your child might do the same.

Stories and parables have the power to communicate memorable, eternal truths that can stick with kids for a lifetime, especially if our own gift of grace and hope is part of the story. As the writer of Hebrews says, "We want each of you to show this same diligence to the very end, in order to make your hope sure. We do not want you to become lazy, but to imitate those who through faith and patience inherit what has been promised" (Hebrews 6:11-13). When darkness threatens to engulf us, these stories of hope will keep us afloat.

The narrative of the nation of Israel is our story. We have all been called by God's grace to follow him in faith to the land he has promised. In the process, we live through ups and downs, times when our faith is strong and times when our faith seems barely alive. We endure hardships and blessings like our predecessors. Their story is ours, and we follow it to its culmination in the life of our Lord and Savior Jesus Christ. The constant references to *hope* and *inheritance* throughout the Old Testament connect all Christians (both Jews and Gentiles) to the hope and heritage of Israel.[8] These suffering people have a name that we share—we have all wrestled with God and come away limping but blessed. By engaging their stories, we walk with God's people through the Old Testament.

By remembering the stories of the civil rights movement under the leadership of Martin Luther King Jr., we walk with the martyrs of that movement. By remembering what happened to Richard Wurmbrand and others, hearing stories of Christ's followers being imprisoned, beaten, and martyred for their faith, we walk alongside them and gain from their experience. True faith breeds true hope, and hope increases our resolve.

We share an identity with suffering people who hope in Jesus Christ. We are the church, those who are "called out."[9] The New Testament writers emphatically repeat that it is important for us to live in a "called out" way before the world.[10] Hope has always characterized the people of God, and the words that described them in the Old Covenant now also apply to the people of God in Christ. If we build on that cornerstone, we will be a people whose holiness is obvious to others because we offer hope in what appear to be hopeless times.

If we are living that way as parents and telling our families what it means, our children will see their own stories as incorporated into the greatest story of all time.

OF HOPE AND HOLINESS

Hope is the light on the pathway to holiness. We have been warned to be sober and to understand the transitory nature of this world. In this state, holiness is a consequence of hope, not a substitute for it.[11] Christians are to prepare themselves for the revelation of Jesus Christ in his glory. They are to do so with "an immediacy that does not attempt to set the time of the end . . . [but] makes the believer ever ready and watchful, moderate and sober."[12] After God gave us a secure salvation and a living hope, he commanded us to "set your hope fully on the grace to be given you when Jesus Christ is revealed" (1 Peter 1:13). We are commanded to bring our desires into conformity with the reality and values of grace.[13]

Those who commit to sharing in the suffering of Christ find that suffering is not judgment, but grace and hope. As Dr. King said, we are "veterans of creative suffering," and we "continue to work with the faith that unearned suffering is redemptive."[14] We raise our children knowing that God has secured a hope for us that will not disappoint, regardless of what life may deal us. Whenever we experience things in life that make us "scrape the bottom," hope will float us to the top.

SETTING OUR HOPE SECURELY

We never know when the course of our lives will change forever. We move along at ease with a particular understanding of the world around us when—*bang!*—something wonderful or horrible happens, and we view the world differently from that moment on. Life changes, plans must be modified, and the world isn't what it used to be. Psychologists call this radical alteration a *discontinuous change*. Our former life has ended, and we are on an entirely new course.

The most emphatic discontinuous change in the history of the world was brought about by the death and resurrection of Christ. The apostle Peter explains that those who are sanctified by Jesus are saved from what they were before because they have been saved from themselves.[15] This perfectly describes those of us who have hope and faith in God. We have been saved from what we would have been without God. This emancipation challenges us to live a unique existence in which circumstances do not determine our response to life.

Hope must be properly placed in order to survive life's great disappointments. People cannot live without hope, so we all hope in something. The question cannot just be, Do you have hope? but, In what are you placing your hope? Do you rest it on something that is certain?

Putting our hope in something fallible is the only thing worse than having no hope at all. When the inevitable tests come, misplaced hope will prove us disappointingly wrong and show that we've wasted precious time and energy on something worthless. No hope or a false hope leaves us speechless when we're called upon to answer the basic questions of our existence. When we have no hope, circumstances determine our attitudes.

Christianity offers us a secure, trustworthy hope that people have relied upon for centuries without being disappointed. We have never heard of anyone who said on his or her deathbed, "I wish I had hoped in something other than God. I wish I had trusted Christ less and relied on my own strength instead." For believers in Christ at the present time, just as it was for each of the men and women of faith listed in Hebrews 11, hope and faith will increase when trouble comes because we understand that God rewards those who seek him and risk what is temporary in order to gain him for eternity.[16]

FAITHFUL BEGINNINGS

Most of us didn't start life with a healthy understanding of hope. Our mothers must not have been thinking when they crooned

Rock-a-bye, baby, on the tree top;
When the wind blows, the cradle will rock;
When the bough breaks, the cradle will fall,
And down will come baby, cradle and all!

Who doesn't know those lyrics? And how is a baby supposed to find comfort in that? Or this:

Now I lay me down to sleep;
I pray the Lord my soul to keep.
If I should die before I wake,
I pray the Lord my soul to take.

"If I should die before I wake . . ."? Unfortunately, we spend a lot of our children's formative years sending them to bed with a nice book, a glass of water, and an unhealthy fear of their potential demise. We're joking a little here, but not that much. If we're going to instill hope in our children, we could start by thinking of some better foundations upon which to build.

Kids are naturally curious about things we'd rather they not ask us about, like death for example. *Where is Grandma? Where's the dog? What will happen to me if I die?* For a lot of kids, sleep is frightening because of this fear, and a lot of adults still struggle with anxiety about the unknown.

We want to teach our kids to be careful. We may hear ourselves saying, "Don't answer the door if it's a stranger." "Don't run out in the middle of the street." If we're not careful, we can instill in our kids a permanent, paralyzing fear. We don't want our kids to be afraid to venture out and take risks.

But what if the cradle falls? What if the worst thing that could happen does happen? What if you die before you wake? What if the nice man with the candy is a predator? How does hope continue in those times?

It is a Christian parent's responsibility to provide the security in which a child's faith and hope can be built. Much of that security comes from the Christian message, which is rooted in the hope that something good can come out of something bad. Sometimes we must hope *in spite of* our current circumstances. That's when an undefined hope becomes Christian hope.

In spite of a shipwreck, God still showed his goodness to the apostle Paul. In spite of Lazarus's death, his family saw him alive again. In spite of the Cross, God defeated death. We hope despite pain and suffering, knowing that God is somehow working this out for his glory and our good.[17] Hope tells us that no matter how bad things get or how dark things appear, "joy comes in the morning" (Psalm 30:5, NKJV). This hope allows us to live with confident, untroubled hearts.[18]

The lullaby we really need for our children is a song of hope in Christ and of an eternity with him that begins when we are reborn into the life of the resurrected Lord. This hope in a risen Savior makes suffering victorious and provides an inheritance that has been ours since the beginning of time.

LEAVEN AND HOLINESS

> Brothers, we do not want you to be ignorant about those who fall asleep, or to grieve like the rest of men, who have no hope. We believe that Jesus died and rose again and so we believe that God will bring with Jesus those who have fallen asleep in him. (1 Thessalonians 4:13-14)

For more than two thousand years, it has been common knowledge that yeast makes dough rise. In Jesus' teachings, the word *yeast* is used in two different ways. In Matthew 16:6, the disciples are cautioned to "be on your guard against the yeast of the Pharisees and Sadducees," meaning that these two groups were often a negative influence. A modern way of saying this might be, "Watch it! One bad apple spoils the bunch!" That's what we usually think of concerning yeast in the Bible.

But Jesus also described the leavening properties of yeast in a very positive way. He once used the illustration of a woman who mixed a small amount of yeast into a massive batch of bread dough to describe the Kingdom of God.[19] We might look at the proportions and say, "There's no way such a tiny amount of yeast is going to leaven such a large batch of dough!" But Jesus says, "Just you wait. Once the yeast is in the dough, it's only a matter of time."

Hope is like the leaven that seeps through the dough and affects every part of it. It appears that the flour and water have overmatched the yeast, but this is not the case. Yeast works in silent, unseen ways. The woman "hides" the yeast in the dough, so you can't necessarily tell it's there. It's like a seed that has fallen into the crack of a sidewalk. You wouldn't think that something so small could eventually tear up a whole street, making a mess of concrete and asphalt. But once the seed is in the ground, it's only a matter of time. Out of the dark crevice it shoots up a tiny sprout, and then a tender leaf. Soon it's time to get the sidewalk and the road fixed!

In the same way, hope works its way through our deepest questions:

"Billions of people have died in the course of history, and you're telling me that this one death is going to make a difference?"

"Look at how dark our world is. How can one event have that much effect?"

"The church can't compete with the world. Christians can't compete with culture. How are we supposed to leaven the whole thing? Hollywood? Wall Street? Capitol Hill?"

The Christian community may look small and outnumbered, but once we get into the world, it's just a matter of time. The world doesn't stand a chance because the One who is in us is greater than the one who is in the world. We have nothing to fear. Our marching orders are clear: Take the message of hope into the world and advance the borders of God's kingdom.

We can make a difference and leave the world a better place than we found it. We'll do it one pinch of yeast and one seed at a time.

In 1966, Martin Luther King Jr. had just given up the $54,123 that accompanied his Nobel Peace Prize. Instead of providing a more financially secure life for his children, he moved his family to the slums of Chicago to live in solidarity with suffering African-American people. His kids weren't even safe playing outside. In place of earthly security, King gave them a bold heritage and a real reason to hope. In 1968, he lost his life for his dream, but the dream didn't die. We are closer now to realizing that dream than we were forty years ago. We still have a long way to go, but there has been progress. There is still reason to hope in that cause.

The primary basis for our hope is the historical fact of the resurrection. We say that King lost his life, but he didn't; really, he found it. He is no more dead than Jesus is dead. When Jesus died, they put him in the ground, but as with any good seed, that's when the real growth began. He was just getting started, and the grave didn't stand a chance.

Once the seed is in the ground, it is only a matter of time. The God of hope, yeast, and seed says that dead things don't stay dead. God promises to restore and redeem, and he isn't finished yet. What are you afraid of? Get out in the world and turn some things right side up!

Take your kids with you.

And "may the God of hope fill you with all joy and peace as you trust in him, so that you may overflow with hope by the power of the Holy Spirit" (Romans 15:13).

In 1967, on radio stations all over the world, the Beatles made a definitive statement to Western culture: "All you need is love." That's pretty gutsy, if you think about it. "All" is very inclusive, but the Beatles' brand of love didn't put bread on the table, walk the dog, pick the kids up from school, do the laundry, or wash the dishes.

Maybe the Beatles were wrong. Two decades later, pop-music sentimentality about love apparently shifted. In another gutsy song, Tina Turner belted out, "What's love got to do with it? What's love, but a second-hand emotion?" People backed her skepticism by making the song number one on the pop charts for three weeks. By the fourth week, though, those bold questions were just an echo in the history of rock and roll.

So is love the cure-all, or is it useless and outdated? These two songs may not really demonstrate a massive cultural shift on the subject of love. What they do indicate, though, is that when it comes to love, our attitudes and feelings go from one extreme to the other, and we may be clueless about what love really is.

Often love is invoked as the rationale for our behavior: Are you doing it out of love? This suggests that love is the bar by which motives can be judged.

A friend might ask, "Do you love her?" as if love is what validates a relationship. If this perception of love is the standard for measuring success in a relationship, then the relationship is running on only half its cylinders. For every two couples who walk down the aisle in America, another couple is signing divorce papers.

"We've fallen out of love," says a wife, explaining why she and her husband separated.

"We just share space," claims a husband, attempting to explain his marriage of convenience.

Does love add any permanence to relationships? Should it? Is it as unreliable as our divorce rate would imply?

Perhaps the problem with love is more in our definition than in our application.

This isn't a book about spouses; it's a book about parenting. Still, much of the love that we give to our kids overflows from the loving foundation of our marriages. Even if you're a single parent, the quality of your relationships with other adults greatly influences the lessons you instill in your children. It is vital for every married parent to live with integrity as a spouse, and for every single parent to invest in honorable relationships. Of course, it's essential that all of our relationships flow from our primary love relationship with God.

With that in mind, let's talk about the subject of love *as parents.* Should love alone be the measuring rod for successful parenting? That would be a switch, wouldn't it? Rather than asking ourselves if we've "raised our kids right," we might ask ourselves how well we have loved them.

That shifts the focus considerably, doesn't it? Asking such a question means focusing less on our kids and more on ourselves. You may not even want to ask yourself the question because it's so difficult to answer. It seems so intangible. It's much easier to show everyone what an obedient child you've produced. You can brag about grade point averages, college acceptance letters, trophy cases, and clean rooms. Or maybe you can't. *Maybe you shouldn't.*

The point is that it may be more important to measure how well you love your children than how well your children behave. It might be the most important thing.

LOVE: THE DEFINITION

Love is complicated. It is a verb, an adjective, and a noun. It is a feeling, a commitment, an invitation, and a boundary. People steal for love and kill for love. Love is inescapable. Like it or not, various people are going to cast their versions of love upon you throughout your life. Whether in bold-lettered headlines or in a sweet letter from Grandma, the various definitions of love will imprint our lives from birth to death. Mothers love their babies, children love their mothers, and almost everyone loves their grandparents. No one doubts that love is an important part of our everyday lives.

Because love plays such a vital role in our existence, shouldn't we be more clear on the subject? Where does love come from? What does love look like? What exactly is it?

Max, an eight-year-old boy, says of the family gerbil, "I love Shorty."

Six-year-old Jessica remarks, "I love Ethan," a friend in her Sunday school class.

Jaime, who is four, defines love as "the feeling when your puppy licks your face even after you left him alone all day."

What about these statements?

"I love Harry Potter."

"I love ice cream."

"I love going to the mall."

"I love that movie."

What do we mean when we say *love?*

How we express love to our children is arguably the most important consideration in parenting. Before defining it, perhaps we should back up a step and ask, Who is so significant that he has the authority to make such a definition? Who is so mighty that she gets to put the words in *Webster's* dictionary next to the "love" entry? If each of us were to write down our definitions of love, there would be as many definitions as writers. There would be some similarities and a lot of differences between definitions. It's the sort of thing that keeps musicians and poets in business.

Perhaps the ultimate definition of love should not be in the hands of wishy-washy individuals such as ourselves who feel warm and fuzzy one day and cold and prickly the next. Maybe someone who can be objective should define this all-important matter. If only the One who created love would speak up, define it, and model it for us so that we could really understand what it is. . . .

Thankfully, he has. God has graciously provided all we need to know about love. We'll explore his definition shortly, but first let's look at one of our most common misunderstandings about love.

MY BIG FAT GREEK LOVE

Our American understanding of love is not something that was invented by Hollywood in the last century. The idea that love is an enchantment completely beyond our control began long ago. The ancient Greeks experienced passionate feeling and believed it was divine madness. If you "fell in love," you could be sure that one of the gods (usually Aphrodite) had visited you and put you under a spell. The divine madness of love caused you to think and act irrationally. Love was supposedly an irresistible force, and humans were helplessly captivated by its seductive sway.

Many today continue to understand love as the Greeks did. If you've ever seen a teenager who claims to be in love, you've witnessed its "spell." He can't eat; she can't sleep. They're starry-eyed, and their sentences are incoherent. They walk around in a daze, as if they've been zapped by some inexplicable insanity. (Some adults behave the same way.)

It is true that feelings of love can be overwhelming. The passion, the romance, the "Romeo and Juliet" of it all are what most people think of when they hear the word. It means sonnets, flowers, and sparks of electricity; it is a ferocious emotion that makes grown men cry and strong men weak. It's a powerful sensation in the pit of the stomach that often drives intelligent people to behave in unintelligent ways. The entire greeting-card industry (not to mention daytime television) is built on this concept of love.

Is love just a powerful feeling? Can love be explained away as an illness or madness—divine or demonic—over which we have no control?

THE HIS-STORY OF LOVE

The Greeks were on to something, but the extreme they chose reflects the fall of humankind in the Garden of Eden. When God breathed life into humans, Adam and Eve lived together without their nakedness being an issue. Scripture says, "The man and his wife were both naked, and they felt no shame" (Genesis 2:25). This may refer to more than physical nudity. It also suggests a kind of transparency in which encouragement and acceptance were the norm and shame and embarrassment never entered their minds. Could this be a picture of God-birthed love in its purest form?

Then it all ended, as we read in Genesis 3. A not-so-divine madness set in as the man claimed that the woman had tricked him into doing something he didn't want to do. She said the serpent had seduced her, and she couldn't help acting irrationally. They threw on some clothes and went into hiding from God and from each other. Ever since then, humans have walked around in a stupor, as if zapped by madness.

Christians realize that God created individuals with the ability to make choices. Love should never be an excuse for being out of control. Being bitten by the "love bug" is never a justification for immoral behavior, even if we felt we just couldn't help ourselves. Love is more than a physical desire or craving.

Still, this idea has sunk its roots deep into our understanding. Sigmund Freud created an entire psychological system about love, the core of which revolved around the natural sexual impulse. All impulses, according to Freud, are sexual impulses. According to him, friendliness and affection are all just facades over a real sexual craving. The raw biological need to procreate may manifest itself in a tempered way, but what we think of as love is really just a desire to propagate our species. The sexual revolution of the late 1960s and early 1970s, with its bewildered understanding of "free" love, expressed this idea rather loudly: "It's just sex. It's natural, man."

Many of our modern theories give a different account of love's origin, but most reach the same flawed conclusion: that love equals physical desire. For those who view love as nothing more than a biological or chemical process, it's all about the pursuit of pleasure—a quest to satisfy the self. As a result, love is "real" only as it relates to our feelings of satisfaction. There is no room in this definition for anything beyond self-interest.

SATURDAY MORNING HARPOONS

The idea that satisfying the self is all-important isn't just being marketed to adults. Those of you who have watched Saturday morning cartoons and the accompanying commercials with your kids have witnessed some serious strategic marketing. Perhaps you don't realize that entire marketing firms exist for the purpose of helping merchandisers make your kids "love" things that they previously didn't even know existed. Frequently, a key strategy is having a little girl announce that she absolutely "loves!" a certain cereal, toy, video game, or movie. You may notice that the average age of the kids in the commercials is just slightly older than the average age of the targeted customers.[1]

What is all this about? Perhaps it's a throwback to Adam and Eve, with a tip of the hat to Freud. On a very simple level, pitches that appeal to our kids' desires to have what is cool, desirable, or meant for an older kid inspire children to beg Mom and Dad for that product. After the first no, the coercion ensues: "But I *looooove* it! I *neeeeed* it!" In short, Hollywood and Madison Avenue have just thrown a harpoon into your family's definition of love (and maybe a wrench into your plans for a happy day and a balanced bank account).

How do we respond as parents? Do we automatically take out the credit card and purchase the desired item? If we do, we may communicate that love equals instant gratification. Do we deny our children their desires no matter how hard they beg? This may convey the idea that love equals never getting what you want.

And you thought parenting would be easy?

Obviously, this is not an exhaustive study of the various philosophies of love.[2] Neither is it a documentary on the commercial invasion of our homes.[3] But with all the bad definitions of love that pervade our society, it's easy to become confused. Maybe our children don't have a coherent idea of love because one isn't being presented.

Should we hate the world for its marketing schemes and bad psychology?

Probably not. After all, how is the world supposed to know what love is?

Could it be that the Hollywood definition of love is so prevalent because there is no alternative vying for attention?

Maybe the problem isn't with them out there, but with us in here.

LOVING OUR BROTHERS

For years, Dick Staub hosted a nationally syndicated radio show. One day he shared with his listeners an interesting story he had come across in an Ann Landers column:

> Her column that morning told the story of a young man named Bob who was about to be married. Bob was asking if he should un-invite his father Jim's "significant other" from the wedding ceremony. Fourteen years earlier, Jim had announced that he was gay and left Bob's mother. Jim now lived with Greg, a kind and thoughtful person. Bob struggled with his father's decision. Though he didn't approve of his father's choice, Bob had come to accept him. On occasion, Bob and his fiancée, Carol, socialized with Jim and Greg.
>
> When Carol's parents heard about this gay union, they were extremely upset and demanded that Greg not attend the wedding. When Greg learned of the situation he said that he understood and that he would voluntarily withdraw from the event. But Bob's dad was deeply offended and asked his son to reconsider.
>
> You be the judge. What would you do in this situation?

The calls came fast and were intense.

"The bride's parents are being ridiculous. If Bob and his fiancée let her parents make this decision, they'll never stop interfering in this marriage."

"Bob's dad is just reaping the benefits of his sinful act. First he leaves his wife, and then he takes up with a man. He should get over his hurt and accept the consequences of his own actions."

"I think what Greg is doing is admirable—this couple should accept his peacemaking offer as a wonderful gift."

Then Pete from Long Beach called. Not only should they tell Greg not to attend, but they should make sure that only born-again Christians attended their wedding.

"And why is that?" I asked.

"Marriage is a Christian ceremony, a sacrament, and we shouldn't pollute it with the presence of unbelievers."

"Sounds like a pretty radical position to me!"

"That's your problem, Dick, you don't understand the importance of separation from the world."

"Really! Tell me more."

"The Bible makes it clear. We are to have no fellowship with darkness. Friendship with the world is enmity with God. Dick, if you believe this, why do you do movie reviews every Thursday on your show?"

"And what do movie reviews have to do with it?"

"We're not supposed to love the world or the things of the world. The world is polluted with sin, and God is going to destroy it anyway! Movies are of the world! We shouldn't waste our time talking about them, and Christians certainly shouldn't be watching them."

"Pete, just so I'm sure I understand you, would you invite movie-going Christians to your wedding, or are they on the non-invite list with all the gays and non-Christians?"

"A real Christian wouldn't go to the movies, but you know

what, Dick? You're a jerk, and I don't want to waste any more time putting my pearls in front of swine like you."

Click. Pete hung up.[4]

How do we respond to a situation like this? Let's start with the Bible: "Do not love the world or anything in the world. If anyone loves the world, the love of the Father is not in him. For everything in the world—the cravings of sinful man, the lust of his eyes and the boasting of what he has and does—comes not from the Father but from the world. The world and its desires pass away, but the man who does the will of God lives forever" (1 John 2:15-17).

Well, that sounds pretty clear, doesn't it? "Do not love the world or anything in the world." Case closed, right? Except for one thing: "God so loved the world that he gave his one and only Son, that whoever believes in him shall not perish but have eternal life" (John 3:16).

That muddies things up a bit. God loves the world, but he calls us not to? That doesn't make much sense. It certainly didn't make sense to William Law, an eighteenth-century writer: "If I hate or despise any man in the world, I hate that which God cannot hate, and despise that which He loves. . . . There is no greater sign of your own baptism in the Spirit than when you find yourself all love and compassion toward them that are very weak and sinful, and especially towards those who oppose or misuse you."[5]

There must be a deeper answer.

The Bible uses the word *world* in several different ways. Sometimes it means this physical planet, whereas at other times it means the place where people live and do business.[6] One definition reflects that which God longs to save, while another characterizes whatever actively opposes God.[7] The word is sometimes understood as a transitory era that is destined to pass away, whereas the eternal paradigm tells us that the Lord will redeem and redefine it.[8]

God loves his creation, and he calls us to share his perspective. God does not love human rebellion, but he does love the humans who so often rebel. It's a good thing that he does, because we've all rebelled against him to varying degrees.[9] Certainly there are people and systems in our world that actively oppose the truth of God. If God is concerned about redeeming and redefining these people and systems, Christians should be morally and culturally engaged. But where do we begin?

THE MUSIC OF LOVE AND PEACE

If we want to demonstrate love to our kids, we are not without a model. The Scriptures tell us:

> Dear friends, let us love one another, for love comes from God. Everyone who loves has been born of God and knows God. Whoever does not love does not know God, because God is love. This is how God showed his love among us: He sent his one and only Son into the world that we might live through him. This is love: not that we loved God, but that he loved us and sent his Son as an atoning sacrifice for our sins. Dear friends, since God so loved us, we also ought to love one another. No one has ever seen God; but if we love one another, God lives in us and his love is made complete in us. (1 John 4:7-12)

> If I speak in the tongues of men and of angels, but have not love, I am only a resounding gong or a clanging cymbal. If I have the gift of prophecy and can fathom all mysteries and all knowledge, and if I have a faith that can move mountains, but have not love, I am nothing. If I give all I possess to the poor and surrender my body to the flames, but have not love, I gain nothing.

> Love is patient, love is kind. It does not envy, it does not boast, it is not proud. It is not rude, it is not self-seeking, it is not easily angered, it keeps no record of wrongs. Love does not delight in evil but rejoices with the truth. It always protects, always trusts, always hopes, always perseveres.

> Love never fails. (1 Corinthians 13:1-8)

These two passages give us a simple way to approach a biblical understanding of love. Though 1 Corinthians 13 is a melodious rendering of how love appears in action, 1 John 4 gives great insight into what love is made of.

One of a guitarist's first lessons is how to tune his instrument. Some use a pitch pipe, and others use electronic tuners with lights and meters. The higher-priced, electronic tuners are probably more precise, but either method allows one to check individual strings with a fair amount of precision. Once the low E-string of a guitar is tuned correctly, the others can easily be adjusted. All guitarists learn this critical discipline because regardless of the musician's skill, an out-of-tune guitar can only make noise. If just one of the six strings is out of tune with the others, the whole thing sounds terrible.

Our children have heartstrings, and we are the tuning tools. If we hope to be accurate tuners, we must first let God manufacture love in us. When he does, we will love without our own agendas and extend the grace that has been extended to us. Though it's often the hardest place to practice it, this love needs to show up in our homes first.[10] Husbands and wives experiencing marital tension might prefer to separate; but they manifest love when they show it to the "neighbor" they married. The wife whose husband has "fallen out of love" and left her for someone new demonstrates love to her children as she loves the "enemy" who used to be her spouse.

All that we know about love comes through God loving us first. His love is revealed in the redemption we are offered in Jesus Christ and in how we interact with each other. When we taste the fullness of God's love, we are compelled to enjoy it and share it with others.

In the last few chapters, we have talked about how Christians should actively engage the culture, understanding that our work amounts to much more than rearranging deck chairs on the Titanic. Our labor for eternal values requires active participation in bringing the mighty peace of God to this world by working with God to set things right. Maybe we can't track our parenting success or brag about GPAs and trophies, but we can parent with the confidence that we're participating in what is most important to God: loving his children.

Our children should get good grades and excel in extracurriculars. They should be the best students and the hardest-working athletes. They should be the most creative artists and the most innovative technicians. But these things are not the goal—they result from the greater goal of being transformed into the image of the One who created our minds, bodies, and spirits. As we are individually transformed and as we help our children in this process, we advance the borders of God's kingdom.

In so doing, we begin a grassroots movement that successfully influences our culture with a God-based philosophy of love and a generation of kids who model it. We tune our instruments and play the irresistible song of God's amazing grace.

LOVE LEADS TO REFORM

As we have seen, stories of great men and women effectively show our kids how genuine love can lead to reform in society. There have always been people of God, such as Wilberforce and King, who loved the people of this world so much that they were willing to give their lives to change things for the better. Elizabeth Fry is another fantastic example.

Elizabeth Fry was born into a wealthy English family in 1780. When she was fifteen years old, she walked past a notorious women's prison and watched the inmates desperately reaching through the bars, begging for help. After she returned home and compared the terrible conditions of those women with her own comfortable surroundings, she wrote in her journal: "If this is the world, where is God?"

Two years later, an American minister named William Savery convinced Elizabeth that God was real and wanted to help others through her. She determined to be God's hands and feet in the broken lives of people such as the poor women she had seen in the prison. She was inspired by Jesus' teaching that whatever we do for the least among us, we do for him.[11] She started a school to educate poor children and give them skills for finding employment. She arranged for medical care and the distribution of food, clothing, soap, and Bibles.

In 1813, Elizabeth heard about Newgate Prison for Women. Nearly three hundred women were crammed into two large cells. Hardened criminals mixed with women who had been convicted of minor offenses, had gotten into debt they couldn't repay, or were still awaiting trial. Violent, mentally imbalanced, destitute, and innocent women (and their children) were all milling about in the same filthy, overcrowded facility.

There was no medical care. More than five women and children died each month, many of starvation. They had no clothing except what they wore when they arrived. There were no beds, pillows, heating systems, or baths, and there was nothing to occupy their time except crying, fighting, and shouting out to people who walked past.

Elizabeth Fry went to see this place for herself. The authorities refused to let her inside, but she was unrelenting. When she finally gained entrance, she was surrounded by the curious inmates. She told them that God sent his Son, Jesus, into a world filled with people exactly like them. She said that Jesus hadn't come to condemn them, but to help them and offer them hope. Jesus had come because he loved them, and she had come for the same reason.

That first visit inspired Elizabeth Fry. She saw how moved the women and children were by God's message of faith, hope, and love. She returned again and again. She set up a school for the children. She enlisted the help of other Christians in providing medical supplies, beds, clothes, and soap. They taught the women the Bible and trained them in marketable skills so they could reduce their debts. They treated the women with respect, as people who mattered to God.

Slowly things began to change. One by one, the inmates turned their lives over to God. England watched, astonished. Elizabeth Fry was invited to go from prison to prison throughout all of Great Britain, instituting reform and introducing the gospel. Then she was invited to go to other countries. Governments passed laws requiring humane treatment of prisoners. God only knows how many lives were irrevocably changed because of one woman's commitment to showing God's love to the least among us.[12]

LOVE AT YOUR HOUSE

How do you bring that kind of love in action to your house? If the best defense is a good offense, then we are in excellent shape. In the command to love our neighbors as ourselves, God has given us a great strategy for helping our children to understand love.[13] As the Scriptures and Elizabeth Fry's example show us, love is not passive. Because we are in God and God is in us, the most natural thing is to let him draw our attention to the needs around us that we can meet as a family. When we get to know our neighbors and find ways to increase their well-being, we plant seeds in the fertile soil of our kids' hearts. Modeling love as a household doesn't have to be overtly spiritual: "Suppose a brother or sister is without clothes and daily food. If one of you says to him, 'Go, I wish you well; keep warm and well fed,' but does nothing about his physical needs, what good is it?" (James 2:15-16).

One of the greatest ways to define love for our children is to live it in practical, everyday ways. Simple things such as helping our neighbors with their yards or handing out popsicles to kids on the first day of school can identify our families as being interested in the lives of others. Baking holiday treats and delivering them to our neighbors as a family can open doors that might close in the faces of strangers who come knocking with a gospel message. You can't love your neighbors if you don't know them.

Loving our neighbors in practical ways can be a profound Christian witness to them; it is also a witness and a learning opportunity for our kids. When we pray with our children for the people next door, it's going to mean a lot more if we've all been over to their house together. This is one way to love our neighbors and our kids.

THE TENSION OF TOLERANCE

We aren't naive, and we don't go to the neighbors' houses blindfolded. It's possible, even likely, that lifestyles in our neighborhoods run contrary to the values we're instilling in our kids. Some of us live in neighborhoods with violence, racial tension, homosexual lifestyles, and other unique challenges. Love is strong enough to grow even in this environment, but there are a few things to think about as we attempt to plant it.

Many Christians withdraw because the head-on collision of values between home and next door (or school, for that matter) is just too much to handle. We are dumbfounded when our neighbor categorizes us as "fundamentalist." We don't have an answer for the relativists who disseminate a new definition of tolerance and then won't tolerate anyone who doesn't accept their new definition.

Previous generations have defined tolerance as accepting the differences between individuals and agreeing to disagree. Neighbors and nations have been allowed the legal freedom to practice the religion of their choice. We should always show respect to others, even when we think their beliefs are wrong. However, it is not intolerant to tell someone that your own beliefs are different from theirs. Tolerance can encompass disagreement and the belief that one opinion corresponds more closely to reality than another. There always has been and always should be tolerance of differences in matters of taste.

But today's tolerance goes beyond accepting another person's right to be wrong; it says that we must embrace the other person's position as if it were our own. It insists that we must never, ever call the beliefs of others false or untrue. If we do, we are conceited, prejudiced, intolerant extremists. Tolerance no longer means accepting someone else's right to be wrong; it means embracing their views and denying that there *is* such a thing as wrong.

Without considering the implications of such beliefs, some Christians like to think of themselves as tolerant people. That's why religious pluralism has become so fashionable. Some people believe that the only choices are between loving others as Jesus did (and embracing their beliefs as well) or not loving others at all. Those with this mind-set feel generous when they say, "Chinese food or French cuisine, Jesus or Nostradamus, permed or straight, life or death are all the same. What you choose does not matter, only your freedom in choosing."[14]

As Christian parents, we are charged with teaching our children how to navigate the tensions of love and truth. Contrary to the new definition of tolerance, we need to help others understand the consequences of a life lived apart from God.

Remember those neighbors to whom you built a bridge with service and a smile? Let love keep you walking toward them in faith, facing fears and going the final stretch. Because friends are an important priority to your kids, shouldn't they be to you too? If you're concerned about what happens at a house one of your children visits, open your door and make your home an inviting alternative. When you're getting ready to grill some hot dogs, throw on an extra batch and invite a mixture of friends from church and outside of church to join you. As God leads you in these endeavors, invite a neighbor or friend to a church service or another event that will expose him or her to the truth of Christ.

Loving God and loving others as a family will become a ministry in itself. It will redefine what the world regards as normal, and it will separate your home in the way that God intended—as a light shining in the darkness.

When your whole household follows Jesus by intentionally living God's love, it will bear fruit. The Bible is filled with stories about Jesus, Paul, and others who converted thousands of formerly deceived people. Although our world's understanding of religion has changed significantly, the same basic principles of salvation stand true: *Jesus is the way and the truth and the life. No one comes to the Father except through him.*[15] This is the bedrock of our faith in Jesus Christ, and abandoning it means abandoning him. Love will allow this truth to flow from us in any way possible.

AND THEY ALL LOVED HAPPILY EVER AFTER

We are just beginning to glimpse why loving hearts were so important to Jesus. In his ministry, he corrected the Pharisees' misguided understanding of a living faith. What Christians do to show love is important, but it is not as important as how they do it. If we engage society with an arrogant attitude in the name of love, we will do more harm than good.

Our kids are watching and listening, ready to take their cues from us. If we want them to grasp what love is, then we must engage the world in loving ways. This means checking our involuntary habits, whether it's our attitude when driving around a crowded parking lot or the unloving comments we make during the evening news about "those people." You might even ask your kids to hold you accountable when your words or demeanor seem out of character with the type of family you intend to be.

Love is most concerned with the redemption of others. Sometimes this involves standing with conviction and telling someone the hard truth, but more often it means entering another person's world in order to invite them into God's world. This means being constantly on the lookout for opportunities to build other people up rather than put them down. This includes our children, who must be nurtured in love and affection if they are to grow into emotionally balanced adults who are able to survive in society and influence it for good.

When a husband and wife love and accept each other, they can teach their children love and acceptance. If disagreements are handled in such a way that both adults treat each other with dignity as they work things out, children will feel more secure when they face tension in their own lives. In this atmosphere of agreeable disagreement, love will prepare them to help others through awkward and stressful crises.

At some point, our children will face discouragement. They will be opposed by the devil, by the forces of this present darkness that oppose God's agenda, and probably by some of their Christian peers. The hope of God that is rooted in his love will sustain them and carry them forward in the task of reaching the entire world with the gospel message. There is no denying that a war is going on. It is bigger than the war on drugs and more divisive than the war on terror. It is a culture war, and we are engaged in it.

What will win the culture war? It isn't violent rhetoric or legislating a Christian agenda, but the sacrificial love of our response to God. The more we understand his concern for us, the richer our attitudes will be toward others, whether a spouse, family member, friend, the spiritually lost, or even our enemies. Hate is focused on the past, but love moves the world forward.

So maybe the Beatles were on the right track. All you need *is* love—a particular kind of love that will allow us to live with all kinds of people and yet hold fast to the truth that will save them; a love that will make us lights to the world. As we love people in this way—by exhibiting the unconditional love of Christ—we will win the hearts of our children and our neighbors.

If you've made it this far, congratulations! The concepts we've discussed in this book can be a little intimidating. We hope we've done more than just talk about some interesting ideas and tell some funny stories. We hope we've given you something practical to do. Our goal was to show how we can live as parents so our children will develop a Christlike character and advance the borders of God's kingdom in their generation.

In this final chapter, we want to offer you hope and encouragement. We believe you can do a great job of parenting. God believes you can do this, and we hope you will believe it too.

YOU CAN DO IT . . . IF YOU ACT LIKE THE GROWN-UP

Your kids don't need you to be their buddy, their teacher, or their coach. They probably don't want you to treat them as peers or involve them in every decision you make. In survey after survey, kids say that what they want from their parents is some parenting. In other words, your kids want you to be the grown-up. Someone's got to be the grown-up in your house, and it should probably be you.

Being a grown-up means doing grown-up things. Grown-ups do what they say they're going to do, and they do things no one else wants to do. Grown-ups work, pay the bills, set boundaries, establish consequences, and enforce discipline. If you want to know how to live as a parent, start here. Keep your word. Get a job. Pay your bills. Establish household rules that have logical consequences. If and when a child steps out-of-bounds, allow those consequences to teach your child. It's not so hard; billions of people have done it for thousands of years.

You can do that, right?

YOU CAN DO IT . . . IF YOU TAKE YOUR TIME

Kids need your presence. "Quality time" is a myth. Quality time cannot be scheduled into your calendar alongside the rest of your meetings: *Monday—Quality Time w/ Kids—7:00 P.M.–7:20 P.M.* It doesn't work like that. One way to spell love for your children is *t-i-m-e.*

There's not enough time in our schedules to get everything accomplished. If you attend every meeting, complete every assignment, meet with every person who wants to see you, and return all your phone calls, you will never leave the office. We haven't even mentioned going to the gym. After you pry yourself away from work, you will sit in traffic. You may listen to a book on tape or talk on your cell phone. Then you might sit in the driveway of your own home waiting for someone to get off the phone so you can go in and join your family for dinner, which is already in progress. In the evening, you will have many other demands on your time. Something has to give (hint: it should not be your family).[1]

One day you will be replaced in your job. Someone else will sit in that office and call those clients. You're probably not indispensable—a lot of other people could do your job if something were to happen to you. But you are the only Mom or Dad your child will ever have. Don't cheat your family—go home and spend time with your kids.

You can do that, right?

YOU CAN DO IT . . . IF YOU SET REALISTIC EXPECTATIONS

The Waltons don't live here anymore, and neither do the Cleavers. The times have changed, and if you expect your family to be perfect, you're only going to drive yourself and everyone around you nuts!

Children are going to act like children. Adults are often going to act like children. Newborn babies are going to cry and spit up. Toddlers are going to say no a lot. Teenagers are going to hog the bathroom and break their curfew. Milk will get spilled, and the carpet will get ruined. Siblings will fight, and so will spouses.

You will probably be compared unfavorably to your child's best friend's parents. You will be accused of being unfair and out of touch with reality. Your children will embarrass you in public, and when they reach a certain age, they will find you embarrassing.

Life is not perfect at anyone's house.

If you want to save everyone a lot of headaches and heartaches, do a reality check on your expectations. Do you really believe that your four-year-old daughter is going to take care of your grandmother's antique jewelry box? Maybe you shouldn't give it to her if you're not prepared for it to be damaged. Is your seventeen-year-old son really going to drive the speed limit in a new Camaro? Will a cross-country road trip be the best way to resolve your marital problems? Will your child be able to maintain a decent grade point average while participating in every extracurricular activity under the sun?

The primary reason families experience friction is that we set unrealistic (and often unspoken) expectations for ourselves. When our expectations go unmet, we experience friction. Sometimes we experience World War III.

Your child may not make the honor roll. Your house may not be as clean as your mother's. Your expectations may be unrealistic and in need of an overhaul. Sit down as a family and come up with a list of reasonable expectations. Communicate these expectations often, and determine what will happen if they go unmet.

You can do that, right?

YOU CAN DO IT . . . IF YOU DON'T PAY TOO MUCH ATTENTION TO THE EXPERTS

There are too many people posing as child-rearing experts. "Experts" publish hundreds of books each year and go on television or talk radio to tell you every little thing you're doing wrong. You can't look at a magazine rack at the grocery store without seeing headlines screaming at you:

YOU MAY BE RAISING A SERIAL KILLER!

WHY EVERYTHING YOU'VE EVER HEARD ABOUT PARENTING IS WRONG!

Magazines and television shows are overly dramatic and prey on our natural fears as parents.

It's downright intimidating, and parents who find themselves burdened by unnecessary guilt will second-guess their every decision. Did I discipline too hard? Am I not disciplining enough? Does my child need more toys or a larger allowance? What if I give my kid too much responsibility too soon?

The questions bombard our minds until we're riddled with self-doubt, and it becomes easier to let the experts tell us what to do. We settle for behavior-modification techniques, withdraw from the culture, and live as if ignorance were bliss. We let someone else tell us how to raise our kids because we don't think we're smart enough or good enough to do it ourselves.

Unfortunately, this mentality also comes packaged in a Christian version. There are plenty of pastors and Christian "experts" who will tell you that there is only one way to raise children according to God. They'll tell you how often to spank, how hard to spank, what to spank for, and what to spank with! They'll provide you with charts and anecdotal evidence. They'll spin statistics and pull Bible verses out of context. Like the secular experts, they say, "We know how to do this, and you don't. If you don't do it our way, you are not doing it God's way!" Some of these people have a lot of nerve and not a lot of sense, and they're undermining your parental authority while claiming that they can restore the sanctity of the family.

Don't pay too much attention to them. Read a book, but if it ever tells you there is only one right way to raise every child, put the book down. Listen to others and learn what you can, but never expect someone else to take the place of the Holy Spirit, who provides you with wisdom and grace to live out your calling as a parent.

You can do that, right?

YOU CAN DO IT . . . IF YOU STOP TRYING TO KEEP UP WITH THE JONESES

Do you realize how much frustration you heap on yourself and your family when you compare your situation with someone else's? Most people are perfectly content with their vehicle until someone down the block gets a newer, shinier version of what they drive. Suddenly their own vehicle looks like something they just pulled out of the junk heap. Your neighbor's car has a new car smell, and yours smells like sweaty kids, sour milk, and stale Cheerios.

You were perfectly happy taking your annual trip to Disney with the kids—until your friend from work announced that this year he's taking his family on a Disney Cruise. Now that's all you can think about. Can you take out a home-equity loan, refinance your gigantic new SUV (the one that you had to have because of the people down the block), and save enough to justify taking the kids on a cruise?

We buy things we don't need with money we don't have to impress people we don't even like. It's madness! We're mortgaging the financial future of our children because we're jealous of what the neighbors have. Remember the part about acting like grown-ups? Apply that here.

Imagine what would happen if we all decided to go out in the yard right now, face the houses to our right and to our left and announce in a voice loud enough for God and everyone to hear: "I quit. You win."

You can do that, right?

YOU CAN DO IT . . . IF YOU RELY ON GOD

Being a parent isn't easy. Some days you will feel you've done an adequate job; other days you will fear you're the worst parent in the history of planet Earth. We've all felt like that. And we've all blown it.

God has called you to do something you cannot do in your own strength; He has also promised to provide you with the tools and resources you need to do the job. He has given us "everything we need for life and godliness" (2 Peter 1:3). God never calls you to do anything unless he is prepared to partner with you and equip you to do it. In his covenant-keeping love, he will keep his end of the bargain and do everything necessary to help you hold up your end.

What do you need for proper parenting? Do you need divine assistance? He's given you the Holy Spirit. Do you need wise parenting principles? He's given you the Bible. Do you need someone to partner with you? He's given you an extended family called the church. If you want to be a good parent, start with these simple things: Pray, rely on God, read the Bible, and go to church.

You can do that, right?

YOU *CAN* DO IT

Our children aren't blank slates; they are small people made in the image of an unimaginably complex and beautiful Creator. They are precious and full of potential beyond what we could ask or imagine. They may become a William Wilberforce, an Elizabeth Fry, a Martin Luther King Jr., a Ludwig van Beethoven, a Leonardo da Vinci, or a Cassie Bernall. They may accomplish something we never thought could happen. They are capable of doing great things, and they just may do them. What an honor you've been given by God!

Figure out what you believe and how you're going to hang on to that while your children grow in faith. Give it all you've got. Model Jesus for your children and their friends. Keep your home open to them and respect their uniqueness. Love God with all your heart, soul, mind, and strength, and love your children as yourselves. Seek out the true, the good, and the beautiful. Put your faith into action. Fill your homes with hope and love. Don't let anyone erode your confidence. You have the Holy Spirit inside you to help with this monumental task. With his help, you can do it!

You really can.

Notes

Introduction

1. Gary L. Thomas, *Sacred Parenting: How Raising Children Shapes Our Souls* (Grand Rapids: Zondervan, 2004), 16.
2. Raymond N. Guarendi, *Back to the Family: How to Encourage Traditional Values in Complicated Times* (New York: Villard, 1990), 65.
3. Stuart Hall, personal correspondence with John Alan Turner.

Chapter 1: Parenting in an Age of Specialization

1. Dr. Raymond N. Guarendi, *You're a Better Parent Than You Think! A Guide to Common-Sense Parenting* (New York: Prentice-Hall, 1985), 2.
2. Although this illustration is common, we are indebted to Hal Runkel's book *ScreamFree Parenting* for first introducing the concept to us as it relates to this topic.
3. Philip Yancey, *Finding God in Unexpected Places* (Ventura, Calif.: Vine, 1997), 4–5.
4. See Judges 2:8.

Chapter 2: Faith Development

1. "AP Breaking News," May 26, 2005, http://sfgate.com/cgi-bin/article.cgi?file=/n/a/2005/05/26/sports/s110749D49.DTL
2. Sofia Cavalletti, *The Religious Potential of the Child* (New York: Paulist, 1983), 31.
3. Ibid.
4. Ibid., 31–32.
5. Edward Robinson, *The Original Vision: A Study of the Religious Experience of Childhood* (New York: Seabury, 1983), xiii.
6. Ibid., 35.

7. Ibid.
8. Bob Russell, personal correspondence with John Alan Turner.
9. Jean Piaget, quoted in Annette Hollander, *How to Help Your Child Have a Spiritual Life* (New York: A&W, 1980), 151.
10. Lanny Donoho, personal correspondence with John Alan Turner.

Chapter 3: Teaching as Jesus Taught

1. C. S. Lewis, *The Great Divorce* (New York: Macmillan, 1946), 75.
2. Dallas Willard, *The Divine Conspiracy: Rediscovering Our Hidden Life in God* (San Francisco: Harper, 1998).
3. Jack Mezirow, "Learning to Think like an Adult," in *Learning as Transformation: Critical Perspectives on a Theory in Progress,* ed. Jack Mezirow (San Francisco: Jossey-Bass, 2000), 22.
4. Gordon T. Smith, *The Voice of Jesus: Discernment, Prayer, and the Witness of the Spirit* (Downers Grove, Ill.: IVP, 2003), 77–78.
5. Gary L. Thomas, *Sacred Parenting: How Raising Children Shapes Our Souls* (Grand Rapids: Zondervan 2004), 203.
6. C. S. Lewis, *The Four Loves* (New York: Harcourt, Brace & Jovanovich, 1960), 66.
7. John Ortberg, *Love beyond Reason* (Grand Rapids: Zondervan, 1998), 71.
8. Hal Runkel, *ScreamFree Parenting: Raising Your Kids by Keeping Your Cool* (Duluth, Ga.: Oakmont, 2005), 37.
9. Misty Bernall, *She Said Yes: The Unlikely Martyrdom of Cassie Bernall* (Nashville: W, 1999).
10. Ibid.

Chapter 4: Your Worldview Is Showing

1. This view actually dates back to the Greek philosopher Aristotle, who formulated the notion of the "natural slave." In Aristotle's view, slaves lacked the higher qualities of the soul necessary for freedom. Slavery, then, was not only good for the master, according to Aristotle, it was also good for slaves, who received the guidance and discipline they were incapable of providing themselves.
2. For more on this, see James Orr, *The Christian View of God and the World as Centering in the Incarnation* (Edinburgh: Andrew Eliot, 1893). This book has been through many revisions and reprints, the most recent being *The Christian View of God and*

the World, with a foreword by Vernon C. Grounds (Grand Rapids: Kregel, 1989). See also David K. Naugle, *Worldview: The History of a Concept* (Grand Rapids: Eerdmans, 2002).

3. Sigmund Freud, *New Introductory Lectures on Psycho-Analysis,* W. J. H. Sprott, trans. (New York: Norton, 1933).

4. Hunter Mead, *Types and Problems of Philosophy* (New York: Holt, 1946).

5. H. P. Rickman, "Dilthey, Wilhelm," in *Encyclopedia of Philosophy,* vol. 2, Paul Edwards, ed. (New York: Macmillan, 1967), 404.

6. James W. Sire, *The Universe Next Door* (Downers Grove, Ill.: IVP, 1997), 16.

7. Arthur F. Holmes, *Contours of a Worldview* (Grand Rapids: Eerdmans, 1983), 3.

8. Armand-Nicholi Jr., *The Question of God* (New York: Free Press, 2002), 7.

9. Dallas Willard, *The Divine Conspiracy: Rediscovering Our Hidden Life in God* (San Francisco: Harper, 1998), 307–308.

10. Much of this material is adapted from Michael E. Wittmer, *Heaven Is a Place on Earth* (Grand Rapids: Zondervan, 2004), 21–33.

11. For a more thorough articulation of "worldview confusion," see Norman Geisler and Peter Bocchino, *Unshakable Foundations* (Minneapolis: Bethany, 2001), 55–69.

12. Nicholas Wolterstorff calls these core beliefs *control beliefs,* which are convictions about the sorts of theories we find acceptable. See Nicholas Wolterstorff, "Theology and Science: Listening to Each Other," in *Religion and Science: History, Method, Dialogue,* ed. W. Mark Richardson and Wesley J. Wildman (New York: Routledge, 1996), 98–99. See also Wolterstorff, *Reason within the Bounds of Religion,* 2nd ed. (Grand Rapids: Eerdmans, 1984).

13. See Genesis 1:28.

14. Gnosticism taught that all matter was evil and contaminated. Thus the Gnostics denied not only the goodness of God's creation but also the full humanity of Jesus, believing that a holy God could never become entangled with matter. The earliest form of this heresy was called Docetism, the idea that Jesus only seemed to be human but was really some kind of specter or phantom. For a detailed discussion of Docetism, see Michael E. Wittmer, *Heaven Is a Place on Earth* (Grand Rapids: Zondervan, 2004), 50–68.

15. See Genesis 1:28-31.
16. Henricus Denzinger and Adolfus Schonmetzer, eds., *Enchiridion Symbolorum,* 32nd ed. (Freiburg: Verlag Herder, 1963), item 1783/3002, 587; English translation from Claude Tresmontant, *Christian Metaphysics,* trans. Gerard Slevin (New York: Sheed and Ward, 1965), 54.
17. Louis Berkhof, *Systematic Theology* (London: Banner of Truth, 1939), 129.
18. George Gaylord Simpson, *The Meaning of Evolution* (New Haven: Yale, 1971), 345.
19. Joseph Pohle, *God: The Author of Nature and the Supernatural,* ed. Arthur Preuss (St. Louis: B. Herder, 1912), 8.
20. Langdon Gilkey, *Maker of Heaven and Earth* (Garden City, N.Y.: Anchor, 1965), 4. Gilkey also notes, "Rather, as the foundation upon which all that is Christianly significant about God is based, the idea of the Creator is an indispensable and primary element in any Christian theology." Ibid., 115.
21. See Michael J. Behe, *Darwin's Black Box* (New York: Touchstone, 1996); Phillip E. Johnson, *Darwin on Trial* (Downers Grove, Ill.: IVP, 1993); Lee Strobel, *The Case for a Creator* (Grand Rapids: Zondervan, 2004).
22. Richard Dawkins, *The Blind Watchmaker* (New York: Norton, 1986).
23. This theme has found expression in Christian thought from Origen and Augustine to contemporary writers such as T. F. Torrance and Gilbert Bilezikian.
24. See Genesis 1:28-30; Acts 14:17; 1 Timothy 6:17; James 1:17.
25. See also Habakkuk 3:17-19.
26. See Isaiah 43:7; Romans 11:36; Ephesians 1:12, 14; Hebrews 2:10.
27. "The Shorter Catechism," *The School of Faith,* ed. and trans. T. F. Torrance (London: James Clarke, 1959), 263. The text of the Westminster Shorter Catechism can also be found online at www.shortercatechism.com.
28. Richard Dawkins, *River Out of Eden: A Darwinian View of Life* (New York: HarperCollins, 1995), 133.
29. Cornelius Plantinga Jr., *Not the Way It's Supposed to Be* (Grand Rapids: Eerdmans, 1995), 8.

30. Ibid.

31. Henry Fairlie, *The Seven Deadly Sins Today* (Notre Dame, Ind.: University of Notre Dame, 1979), vii.

32. Plantinga, *Not the Way It's Supposed to Be,* 199.

Chapter 5: Ultimate Reality of Virtual Reality?

1. Os Guinness, *God in the Dark* (Wheaton, Ill.: Crossway, 1996), 57.

2. A. W. Tozer, *The Knowledge of the Holy* (New York: Harper & Row, 1961), 1.

3. George Barna and Mark Hatch, *Boiling Point: It Only Takes One Degree* (Ventura, Calif.: Regal, 2001), 42.

4. The Barna Group, "Born Again Adults Less Likely to Co-Habit, Just as Likely to Divorce," *The Barna Update,* August 6, 2001, http://www.barna.org/FlexPage.aspx?Page=BarnaUpdate&BarnaUpdateID=95.

5. Carmen DeNavas-Walt, Robert Cleveland, and Bruce H. Webster Jr., U.S. Census Bureau, Current Population Reports, P60–221, *Income in the United States: 2002,* U.S. Government Printing Office, Washington DC, 2003, http://www.census.gov/prod/2003pubs/p60-221.pdf.

6. John L. Ronsvalle and Silvia Ronsvalle, *The State of Church Giving through 2001* (Cumberland, Md.: Empty Tomb, 2003), 52.

7. Carol Bellamy, *The State of the World's Children 2001* (UNICEF, 2003), 81.

8. George Gallup Jr., and James Castelli, *The People's Religion* (New York: Macmillan, 1989), 188.

9. Michael O. Emerson and Christian Smith, *Divided by Faith: Evangelical Religion and the Problem of Race in America* (Oxford: Oxford University Press, 2000), 170.

10. See Michael Emerson, "Faith That Separates: Evangelicals and Black-White Race Relations," in Michael Cromartie, ed., *A Public Faith* (New York: Rowman & Littlefield, 2003).

11. We are indebted to Philip Yancey's marvelous book *The Jesus I Never Knew* for this analogy.

12. See John 14:9; Colossians 2:9; Hebrews 1:3.

13. C. S. Lewis, *The Lion, the Witch, and the Wardrobe* (New York: Macmillan, 1970), 76–78.

14. C. S. Lewis, *The Silver Chair* (Middlesex, England: Puffin, 1977), 26–27.
15. Pablo Casals, "You Are A Marvel," in Jack Canfield and Mark Victor Hansen, comp., *Chicken Soup for the Soul* (Deerfield Beach, Fla.: Health Communications, 1993).

Chapter 6: Who, What, Where, When, Why?

1. Bob Nahrstadt, personal correspondence with John Alan Turner.
2. Roger Olson, *The Story of Christian Theology: Twenty Centuries of Tradition and Reform* (Downers Grove, Ill.: IVP, 1999), 477.
3. Kurt Bruner, *I Still Believe* (Grand Rapids: Zondervan, 2005), 20.
4. Maggie Gallagher, quoted in Erin Andersen, "The Culture of Marriage," JournalStar.com, July 29, 2004. Article can be found online at www.journalstar.com/articles/2005/05/15/sunday_am/10052221.txt
5. Maggie Gallagher, testimony on the Marriage Affirmation and Protection Amendment (H3190), Massachusetts Statehouse, April 28, 2003. Transcript of testimony can be found online at www.mafamily.org/Marriage%20Hearing%202003/maggiegallagher.htm
6. www.barna.org/FlexPage.aspx?Page=Topic&TopicID=10

Chapter 7: True vs. False

1. Carlo Collodi, *Pinocchio: The Tale of a Puppet* (Racine, Wisc.: Whitman, 1916), 80.
2. *Webster's New World Dictionary and Thesaurus,* second edition (Cleveland: Webster's New World, 2002).
3. Rubel Shelly, *Written in Stone: Ethics for the Heart* (West Monroe, La.: Howard, 1994), 173–175.
4. Sissela Bok, *Lying: Moral Choice in Public and Private Life* (New York: Pantheon, 1978), 31.
5. See Mark 10:17-22.

Chapter 8: Good vs. Bad

1. Monica Davey, "Secret Passage," *Chicago Tribune* magazine, April 21, 2002, Centre for Counterintelligence and Security Studies, http://www.cicentre.com/Documents/DOC_Hanssen_Tribunemag.htm.

2. Philip Shenon, "Spy Suspect Known for Devout Faith," *Charlotte Observer*, February 25, 2001.
3. Ibid.
4. William Lane Craig, *Reasonable Faith* (Wheaton, Ill.: Crossway, 1994), 73–74.
5. Mead's research has since come under serious scrutiny. Most notably, Derek Freeman's book *Margaret Mead and Samoa: The Making and Unmaking of an Anthropological Myth* (Cambridge, Mass.: Harvard University Press, 1983) has challenged the scholarship and integrity of her research.
6. Jean Bethke Elshtain, "Judge Not?" *First Things* 46 (October 1994): 39.
7. Augustine, *The Confessions of St. Augustine* (Garden City, N.Y.: Image, 1960), 354.
8. See Romans 2:15.
9. These anonymous personal confessions were compiled from www.notproud.com.
10. Francis J. Beckwith and Gregory P. Koukl, *Relativism: Feet Firmly Planted in Mid-Air* (Grand Rapids: Baker, 1998), 166.
11. C. S. Lewis, "The Poison of Subjectivism," in *Christian Reflections*, ed. Walter Hooper (Grand Rapids: Eerdmans, 1967), 77–78. See also J. Budziszewski, *What We Can't Not Know* (Dallas: Spence, 2003).
12. C. S. Lewis, *Mere Christianity* (New York: Macmillan, 1960), 22.
13. See Ephesians 2:10.
14. See Romans 12:2.
15. See John 3:33; Romans 3:4.

Chapter 9: Beautiful vs. Ugly

1. Nicholas D. Kristof, "The Veiled Resource," *New York Times,* - December 11, 2001.
2. Anthony O'Hear, *Beyond Evolution* (Oxford: Clarendon, 1999), 195.
3. Joseph "Skip" Ryan, *Worship: Beholding the Beauty of the Lord* (Wheaton, Ill.: Crossway, 2005), 15.
4. Brian McLaren, personal correspondence with John Alan Turner.
5. This is one reason why fairy tales are good reading for you and your children. Good children's literature introduces them to the

idea of malevolent forces in easy-to-understand ways, training their imaginations so they become people who can steer through the complicated and mysterious waters of morality. For more on this, we recommend Vigen Guroian's *Tending the Heart of Virtue: How Classic Stories Awaken a Child's Moral Imagination* (New York: Oxford University Press, 1998).

6. C. S. Lewis, *The Weight of Glory* (New York: Macmillan, 1949), 1–2.
7. Thomas Dubay, *The Evidential Power of Beauty: Science and Theology Meet* (San Francisco: Ignatius, 1999), 83.
8. For more on this, see Cornelius Plantinga, *Not the Way It's Supposed to Be: A Breviary of Sin* (Grand Rapids: Eerdmans, 1995).
9. See 1 Corinthians 13:12.
10. See Revelation 21:22.
11. See Revelation 21:27.
12. See Colossians 3:2-3.
13. See Mark 13:7-8.
14. See Hebrews 11:1.
15. See Romans 1:18-20.
16. G. K. Chesterton, *Orthodoxy* (San Francisco: Ignatius, 1995), 60.
17. See James 1:17.
18. See Psalm 23:2-3; Genesis 15:5.
19. C. S. Lewis, *Letters to Malcolm: Chiefly on Prayer* (New York: Harvest, 2002), 91.
20. The Barna Group, *Evangelism Is Most Effective among Kids,* October 11, 2004.
21. See Hebrews 4:12.
22. See Colossians 1:15-20.

Chapter 10: Faith

1. See Matthew 3:16; John 3:8; Acts 2:3.
2. See Acts 28:25.
3. See Matthew 4:1; Luke 4:18-19.
4. See John 16:7-15.
5. See Romans 8:6.
6. See Galatians 5.
7. See Romans 5:5.
8. See Ephesians 2:10.

9. See 2 Corinthians 1:21-22; Ephesians 1:13.
10. See Romans 8:1-14.
11. See 1 Corinthians 2:9-11.
12. This idea comes from a message titled "Living a Life of Faith" given by Gordon Straw at the ELCA Churchwide Assembly on August 18, 1999. The transcript is available at http://www.elca.org/assembly99/straw.html.
13. See John 3:5.
14. Straw, "Living a Life of Faith."
15. See Hebrews 6:19.
16. Gary L. Thomas, *Sacred Parenting: How Raising Children Shapes Our Souls* (Grand Rapids: Zondervan, 2004), 49.
17. See John 17:18.
18. See John 14:12.
19. See Romans 12:2; 1 Corinthians 2:6-16.
20. Britannia.com, s.v. "William Wilberforce," http://www.britannia.com/bios/wilberforce.html.
21. Peter Hammond, "Setting the Captives Free," www.frontline.org.za/articles/settingcaptives_free.htm.
22. Ibid.
23. The title of the book was a mouthful: *A Practical View of the Prevailing Religious System of Professed Christians.*
24. For more information, visit the John Newton Project at www.johnnewton.org.

Chapter 11: Hope

1. Martin Luther King Jr., "I Have a Dream" (speech, Lincoln Memorial, Washington, D.C., August 28, 1963).
2. From Amos 5:24, quoted in Martin Luther King Jr., "I Have a Dream."
3. Martin Luther King Jr., "I Have a Dream."
4. Barbara Francis, "Growing Kids God's Way? A Critique of Growing Families International," A Collection of Resources, www.ezzo.info, http://www.ezzo.info/Francis/emotional.htm.
5. Richard Wurmbrand, preface to *Sermons in Solitary Confinement* (London: Hodder & Stoughton, 1969).
6. Leonard Sweet, *Post-Modern Pilgrims* (Nashville: Broadman and Holman, 2000), 87–88.

7. Ibid.

8. J. H. Elliott, *A Home for the Homeless: A Sociological Exegesis of 1 Peter, Its Situation and Strategy* (Philadelphia: Fortress, 1981), 21–58.

9. See 1 Peter 2:9-10; Jude 1.

10. See Galatians 5:13; 2 Timothy 1:9; 1 Peter 1:15.

11. Wolfgang Schrage, *The Ethics of the New Testament,* trans. David E. Green (Philadelphia: Fortress, 1988), 270.

12. Leslie Kline, "Ethics for the End Time," *Restoration Quarterly* 23 (1966): 121.

13. John Piper, "Hope as the Motivation for Love," *New Testament Studies* 26 (1980): 216.

14. Martin Luther King Jr., "I Have a Dream."

15. 1 Peter 2:9-10, 24-25

16. See Hebrews 11:25-26.

17. See Romans 8:28.

18. See John 14:1-3.

19. See Matthew 13:33; Luke 13:20-21.

Chapter 12: Love

1. A PBS *Frontline* documentary, *The Merchants of Cool: A Report on the Creators and Marketers of Popular Culture for Teenagers,* did a fascinating study of this subject. For more information, visit http://www.pbs.org/wgbh/pages/frontline/shows/cool.

2. There are some great studies of love out there. You might want to start with C. S. Lewis, *The Four Loves* (New York: Harcourt, Brace & Jovanovich: 1960).

3. There are also some great studies on this topic. We recommend Craig L. Blomberg, *Neither Poverty nor Riches: A Biblical Theology of Possession* (Downers Grove, Ill.: IVP, 1999).

4. Dick Staub, *Too Christian, Too Pagan* (Grand Rapids: Zondervan, 2000), 34–35.

5. William Law, *The Power of the Spirit* (Fort Washington, Pa.: Christian Literature Crusade, 1971), 123.

6. See Genesis 11:1; 1 Chronicles 16:30.

7. See John 3:16-17; Romans 12:2.

8. See 1 Corinthians 7:31; Revelation 11:15.

9. See Romans 3:23.

10. While we're recommending books, we might as well mention Glenn T. Stanton, *My Crazy Imperfect Christian Family: Living Out Your Faith with Those Who Know You Best* (Colorado Springs: Navpress, 2004).
11. See Matthew 25:31-40.
12. Much of the biographical information here comes from Lee Strobel, "Being a Hero of the Forgotten," message presented at Willow Creek Community Church, July 18, 1998.
13. See Matthew 22:39.
14. Roger Lundin, "The Pragmatics of Postmodernity," in *Christian Apologetics in the Postmodern World*, ed. Timothy R. Phillips and Dennis L. Ockholm (Downers Grove, Ill.: IVP, 1995), 77.
15. See John 14:6.

Conclusion: You Can Do It!

1. For more on this, see Andy Stanley, *Choosing to Cheat* (Sisters, Ore.: Multnomah, 2002).

For Further Reading

Faith, Hope, and Love

Burchett, Dave. *When Bad Christians Happen to Good People: Where We Have Failed Each Other and How to Reverse the Damage.* Colorado Springs: WaterBrook, 2002.

Downs, Tim. *Finding Common Ground: How to Communicate with Those outside the Christian Community . . . While We Still Can.* Chicago: Moody, 1999.

Fernando, Ajith. *Sharing the Truth in Love: How to Relate to People of Other Faiths.* Grand Rapids: Discovery House, 2001.

Fischer, John. *Fearless Faith: Beyond the Walls of Safe Christianity.* Eugene, Ore.: Harvest House, 2002.

Groothuis, Douglas. *Christianity That Counts: Being a Christian in a Non-Christian World.* Grand Rapids: Baker, 1994.

Guinness, Os. *Doing Well and Doing Good: Money, Giving, and Caring in a Free Society.* Colorado Springs: NavPress, 2001.

_____. *Entrepreneurs of Life: Faith and the Venture of Purposeful Living.* Colorado Springs: NavPress, 2001.

_____. *The Great Experiment: Faith and Freedom in America.* Colorado Springs: NavPress, 2001.

_____. *The Journey: Our Quest for Faith and Meaning.* Colorado Springs: NavPress, 2001.

Merrill, Dean. *Sinners in the Hands of an Angry Church: Finding a Better Way to Influence Our Culture.* Grand Rapids: Zondervan, 1997.

Nathan, Rich. *Who Is My Enemy?: Welcoming People the Church Rejects.* Grand Rapids: Zondervan, 2002.

Newman, Randy. *Questioning Evangelism: Engaging People's Hearts the Way Jesus Did.* Grand Rapids: Kregel, 2004.

Schmidt, Alvin J. *How Christianity Changed the World.* Grand Rapids: Zondervan, 2001.

Staub, Dick. *Too Christian, Too Pagan: How to Love the World without Falling for It.* Grand Rapids: Zondervan, 2000.

Zacharias, Ravi. *Deliver Us from Evil: Restoring the Soul in a Disintegrating Culture.* Dallas: Word, 1996.

Parenting and Family

Allender, Dan B. *How Children Raise Parents: The Art of Listening to Your Family.* Colorado Springs: WaterBrook, 2003.

Borba, Michele. *Building Moral Intelligence: The Seven Essential Virtues That Teach Kids to Do the Right Thing.* San Francisco: Jossey-Bass, 2001.

Borsellino, Chuck, and Jenni Borsellino. *How to Raise Totally Awesome Kids.* Sisters, Ore.: Multnomah, 2002.

Boyd, Charles F. *Different Children, Different Needs: Understanding the Unique Personality of Your Child.* Sisters, Ore.: Multnomah, 1994.

Canfield, Ken. *The Heart of a Father: How Dads Can Shape the Destiny of America.* Chicago: Northfield, 1996.

Cline, Foster W., and Jim Fay. *Parenting with Love and Logic: Teaching Children Responsibility.* Colorado Springs: Pinon, 1990.

Elmore, Tim. *Nurturing the Leader within Your Child: What Every Parent Needs to Know.* Nashville: Nelson, 2001.

Fuller, Cheri. *Through the Learning Glass: A Child's Nine Learning Windows You Don't Want to Miss.* Grand Rapids: Zondervan, 1999.

Guarendi, Raymond N. *You're a Better Parent Than You Think!: A Guide to Common-Sense Parenting.* New York: Fireside, 1985.

Guarendi, Raymond N., with David Eich. *Back to the Family: Proven Advice on Building a Stronger, Happier Family.* New York: Fireside, 1990.

Hallowell, Edward M. *The Childhood Roots of Adult Happiness: Five Steps to Help Kids Create and Sustain Lifelong Joy.* New York: Ballantine, 2002.

Kimmel, Tim. *Grace-Based Parenting.* Nashville: W, 2004.

Kohn, Alfie. *Unconditional Parenting: Moving beyond Rewards and Punishments to Love and Reason.* New York: Atria, 2005.

Lickona, Thomas. *Character Matters: How to Help Our Children Develop Good Judgment, Integrity, and Other Essential Virtues.* New York: Touchstone, 2004.

Miller, David R. *Breaking Free: Rescuing Families from the Clutches of Legalism.* Grand Rapids: Baker, 1992.

Runkel, Hal Edward. *ScreamFree Parenting: Becoming the "Cool" Parent Your Kids Really Need.* Duluth, Ga.: Oakmont, 2005.

Shaw, Robert. *The Epidemic: The Rot of American Culture, Absentee and Permissive Parenting, and the Resultant Plague of Joyless, Selfish Children.* New York: Regan, 2003.

Stafford, Tim. *Never Mind the Joneses: Building Core Christian Values in a Way That Fits Your Family.* Downers Grove, Ill.: IVP, 2004.

Stanton, Glenn T. *My Crazy Imperfect Christian Family: Living Out Your Faith with Those Who Know You Best.* Colorado Springs: NavPress, 2004.

Thomas, Gary L. *Sacred Parenting: How Raising Children Shapes Our Souls.* Grand Rapids: Zondervan, 2004.

Turansky, Scott, and Joanne Miller. *Good and Angry: Exchanging Frustration for Character—in You and Your Kids!* Colorado Springs: Shaw, 2002.

_____. *Say Goodbye to Whining, Complaining, and Bad Attitudes—in You and Your Kids!* Colorado Springs: Shaw, 2000.

Whitehurst, Teresa. *How Would Jesus Raise a Child?* Grand Rapids: Baker, 2003.

Yates, John, and Susan Yates. *Building a Home Full of Grace.* Grand Rapids: Baker, 2003.

Truth, Goodness, and Beauty

Buchanan, Mark. *Things Unseen: Living in Light of Forever.* Sisters, Ore.: Multnomah, 2002.

Dubay, Thomas. *The Evidential Power of Beauty: Science and Theology Meet.* San Francisco: Ignatius, 1999.

Guinness, Os. *Steering through Chaos: Vice and Virtue in an Age of Moral Confusion*. Colorado Springs: NavPress, 2000.

_____. *Time for Truth: Living Free in a World of Lies, Hype, and Spin*. Grand Rapids: Baker, 2000.

_____. *When No One Sees: The Importance of Character in an Age of Image*. Colorado Springs: NavPress, 2000.

Kreeft, Peter. *Back to Virtue: Traditional Moral Wisdom for Modern Moral Confusion*. San Francisco: Ignatius, 1992.

Lindsley, Art. *True Truth: Defending Absolute Truth in a Relativistic World*. Downers Grove, Ill.: IVP, 2004.

McGrath, Alister. *The Unknown God: Searching for Spiritual Fulfillment*. Grand Rapids: Eerdmans, 1999.

Shelly, Rubel. *Written in Stone: Ethics for the Heart*. West Monroe, La.: Howard, 1994.

Yancey, Philip. *Rumors of Another World: What on Earth Are We Missing?* Grand Rapids: Zondervan, 2003.

Zacharias, Ravi. *Recapture the Wonder*. Nashville: Integrity, 2003.

Worldview and Apologetics

Colson, Charles, with Harold Fickett. *The Good Life: Seeking Purpose, Meaning, and Truth in Your Life*. Wheaton, Ill.: Tyndale, 2005.

Colson, Charles, and Nancy Pearcey. *How Now Shall We Live?* Wheaton, Ill.: Tyndale, 1999.

Copan, Paul. *How Do You Know You're Not Wrong?: Responding to Objections That Leave Christians Speechless*. Grand Rapids: Baker, 2005.

_____. *That's Just Your Interpretation: Responding to Skeptics Who Challenge Your Faith*. Grand Rapids: Baker, 2001.

_____. *True for You but Not for Me: Deflating the Slogans That Leave Christians Speechless*. Minneapolis: Bethany, 1998.

Geisler, Norman, and Peter Bocchino. *Unshakable Foundations: Contemporary Answers to Crucial Questions about the Christian Faith*. Minneapolis: Bethany, 2001.

Guinness, Os. *Fit Bodies, Fat Minds: Why Evangelicals Don't Think and What to Do about It*. Grand Rapids: Hourglass, 1994.

Herrick, James A. *The Making of the New Spirituality: The Eclipse of the Western Religious Tradition*. Downers Grove, Ill.: IVP, 2003.

Holmes, Arthur. *All Truth Is God's Truth*. Grand Rapids: Eerdmans, 1977.

Lewis, C. S. *Mere Christianity*. San Francisco: Harper, 2001.

_____. *Miracles*. San Francisco: Harper, 2001.

_____. *God in the Dock: Essays on Theology and Ethics*, ed. Walter Hooper. Grand Rapids: Eerdmans, 1970.

Marshall, Paul, with Lela Gilbert. *Heaven Is Not My Home: Living in the Now of God's Creation*. Nashville: Word, 1998.

Moreland, J. P. *Love Your God with All Your Mind: The Role of Reason in the Life of the Soul*. Colorado Springs: NavPress, 1997.

Naugle, David. *Worldview: The History of a Concept*. Grand Rapids: Eerdmans, 2002.

Pearcey, Nancy. *Total Truth: Liberating Christianity from Its Cultural Captivity*. Wheaton, Ill.: Crossway, 2004.

Plantinga, Cornelius, Jr. *Not the Way It's Supposed to Be: A Breviary of Sin*. Grand Rapids: Eerdmans, 1995.

Schaeffer, Francis A. *How Should We Then Live?: The Rise and Decline of Western Thought and Culture*. Old Tappan, N.J.: Revell, 1976.

_____. *The God Who Is There*. Downers Grove, Ill.: InterVarsity, 1998.

_____. *He Is There and He Is Not Silent*. Wheaton, Ill.: Tyndale, 1972.

_____. *Escape from Reason*. Downers Grove, Ill.: IVP, 1977.

_____. *Death in the City*. Wheaton, Ill.: Crossway, 2002.

Sire, James W. *The Universe Next Door: A Basic Worldview Catalog*. 3rd ed. Downers Grove, Ill.: IVP, 1997.

Wittmer, Michael E. *Heaven Is a Place on Earth: Why Everything You Do Matters to God*. Grand Rapids: Zondervan, 2004.

Zacharias, Ravi. *Can Man Live without God?* Dallas: Word, 1994.

_____. *Jesus among Other Gods: The Absolute Claims of the Christian Message*. Nashville: Word, 2000.

About the Authors

Dr. Kenneth Boa is president of Reflections Ministries, an organization that seeks to encourage, teach, and equip people to know Christ, follow Him, become progressively conformed to His image, and reproduce His life in others. Ken is also president of Trinity House Publishers, a publishing company dedicated to the creation of tools that will help people manifest eternal values by drawing them to intimacy with God and a better understanding of the culture in which they live.

Ken holds a B.S. from Case Institute of Technology, a Th.M. from Dallas Theological Seminary, a Ph.D. from New York University, and a D.Phil. from the University of Oxford in England.

Ken is the author of more than fifty books, including *Conformed to His Image*, *Twenty Compelling Evidences that God Exists*, *Face to Face*, *Augustine to Freud*, and Gold Medallion winners *An Unchanging Faith in a Changing World* and *Faith Has Its Reasons*. He is a contributing editor to *The Open Bible* and *The Leadership Bible*, and a consulting editor for the *Zondervan NASB Study Bible*.

Ken and his wife live in Atlanta, Georgia.

John Alan Turner is president of Faith 2.0, an organization committed to helping people live better lives by reexamining what they really believe. He also works with the reThink Group, providing consulting, curriculum, training, and other resources to more than two thousand churches, schools, and families worldwide. He speaks to thousands of people every year at youth rallies, retreats, and conferences.

John attended Pepperdine University, Pacific Christian College, and the Bear Valley Bible Institute, earning a Th.M. in biblical theology, with special emphasis on New Testament studies. He is currently pursuing a Ph.D. in religion and philosophy.

John writes for 252Basics' Family Production, a family-centered church curriculum that makes learning about faith and character issues fun and relevant. He has also written articles and book reviews for *New Wineskins* magazine and *Integrity Journal*.

John lives in Norcross, Georgia, with his wife, Jill, and their three daughters.

Look for these insightful worldview books by CHARLES COLSON wherever fine books are sold

The Good Life
by Charles Colson with Harold Fickett
Have you found the good life? Charles Colson explains what the *true* good life is.

Also, check out these study resources for *The Good Life*:

The Good Life Discussion Guide
by Charles Colson with Harold Fickett

In Search of the Good Life (booklet)
by Charles Colson with Harold Fickett

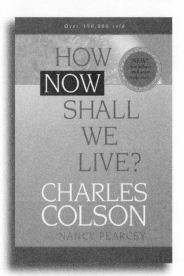

How Now Shall We Live?
by Charles Colson and Nancy Pearcey
The groundbreaking book on the Christian worldview by Charles Colson.

Expose the lies of our culture:

**Lies That Go
Unchallenged:
Popular Culture**

**Lies That Go
Unchallenged:
Media and Government**

Apply the Christian worldview to your life:

**Tough Questions
about God, Faith,
and Life**

Hearts and Minds

**How Now Shall
We Live?
Devotional**

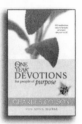

**The One Year Devotions
for People of Purpose**

Developing a Christian Worldview series
Discover *How Now Shall We Live?* worldview issues in a format for individual and group study:

Science and Evolution

The Problem of Evil

**The Christian in
Today's Culture**

A complete *How Now Shall We Live?* adult and youth video curriculum
is available from LifeWay Church Resources:
Customer Services, MSN 113
One LifeWay Plaza
Nashville, TN 37234-0113
Fax: 1-615-251-5933
Catalog orders: 1-800-458-2772
Order from online catalog at www.lifeway.com/shopping